JAY MCCAIG

Making The Bible Clear

How Anyone Can Understand God's Word

**UPRIGHT &
MOVING FORWARD**
PRESS

First edition

ISBN: 979-8-9999656-1-5

This book was professionally typeset on Reedsy.
Find out more at reedsy.com

Contents

V   Next Steps and Resources

Introduction

You're Not as Lost as You Think

Why did you pick up this book? Maybe you've been a Christian for a while, but every time you try to read the Bible, you feel like you're trying to decipher ancient hieroglyphics. Or you're relatively new to the faith and intimidated by that thick book everyone talks about with such reverence. You've heard people confidently quote Scripture and wonder if you'll ever get there yourself.

Here's the truth that might surprise you: feeling lost in the Bible doesn't mean you're not smart enough, spiritual enough, or Christian enough. It means you're human. Even the disciples, who walked with Jesus, struggled to understand Scripture. Remember when Philip encountered the Ethiopian reading Isaiah? The man responded honestly, "How can I, except some man should guide me?" (Acts 8:31).

If a court official who obviously valued Scripture enough to read it while traveling needed help understanding it, you're in pretty good company.

The Myth That's Keeping You Stuck

Somewhere along the way, we've created a myth that the Bible is primarily for pastors, seminary professors, and people who can pronounce "Deuteronomy" without stumbling. This thought couldn't be further from the truth. When Paul wrote to the church in Corinth, he reminded them, "For ye see your calling, brethren, how that not many wise men after the flesh, not many mighty, not many noble, are called: But God hath chosen the foolish things of the world to confound the wise" (1 Corinthians 1:26-27).

God didn't write His Word for the intellectual elite. He wrote it for fishermen, tax collectors, farmers, and regular people trying to figure out how to follow Him. The same God who made His truth clear to them wants to make it clear to you.

Why God Wants You to Understand His Word

Scripture tells us that God desires all His people to know Him through His Word. David declared, "The law of the Lord is perfect, converting the soul: the testimony of the Lord is sure, making wise the simple" (Psalm 19:7). Notice that the word "simple" is not an insult; it's an invitation. God's Word has the power to make wise those who approach it with humble hearts, regardless of their educational background.

Jesus promised His disciples, "But when he, the Spirit of truth, is come, he will guide you into all truth" (John 16:13). That same Spirit lives in every believer today, ready to illuminate God's Word for anyone who asks.

What This Book Will (and Won't) Do

This book won't turn you into a theologian overnight and won't give you ammunition to win every Bible argument at the church potluck. What it will do is give you practical tools to read Scripture with confidence, understand what you're reading, and apply it to your daily life.

You won't need to learn Greek or Hebrew (though we'll talk about when those tools might be helpful). You won't need an expensive library of commentaries to get started. You won't even need to understand every single verse to benefit significantly from God's Word.

What you will need is what you probably already have: a sincere desire to know God better and the humility to learn. As Jesus said, "Blessed are they which do hunger and thirst after righteousness: for they shall be filled" (Matthew 5:6).

Starting Where You Are

Maybe you've tried to read through the Bible before and got bogged down somewhere around Leviticus. Perhaps you've attended Bible studies where everyone seemed to understand things that left you scratching your head. Maybe you've been avoiding Bible study altogether because it feels overwhelming.

Here's your permission to start exactly where you are right now. The woman at the well didn't have a seminary degree, but her encounter with Jesus through God's truth changed her life. The jailer in Philippi probably couldn't quote much Scripture, but when he asked Paul and Silas what he needed to do to be saved, he was ready to listen and learn.

God meets us where we are, not where we think we should be.

Your Guide for the Journey

Think of this book as a friendly guide rather than a textbook. I've been studying and teaching the Bible for over twenty years and still discover new things regularly. The goal isn't to know everything—it's to know how to learn and grow in understanding over time.

We'll start with the basics: what the Bible is, how it's organized, and what tools you actually need (spoiler alert: fewer than you think). Then, we'll move into practical methods that work for real people with real schedules. We'll tackle the difficult passages, the confusing parts, and those Old Testament laws that seem to have nothing to do with modern life.

Most importantly, we'll keep coming back to this central truth: "All scripture is given by inspiration of God, and is profitable for doctrine, for reproof, for correction, for instruction in righteousness: That the man of God may be perfect, thoroughly furnished unto all good works" (2 Timothy 3:16-17). God gave us His Word not to confuse us, but to equip us for the life He's called us to live.

An Invitation, Not an Assignment

Before we dive in, let me clarify something important: Bible study should never feel like a burden or a religious duty you must check off your list. It's an invitation to know the God who loves you enough to reveal Himself through His Word.

Yes, it takes effort—anything worthwhile does. But it's the kind of effort that leads to joy, not drudgery. As the psalmist wrote, "O how love I thy law! it is my meditation all the day" (Psalm 119:97). When we begin to understand

God's Word, it becomes less like homework and more like a conversation with someone we love.

Ready to Begin?

If you're still reading, you're already taking the first step. You have everything you need to begin this journey: a heart that wants to know God better and His Word that's ready to reveal Him to you.

The Ethiopian official's question echoes through the centuries: "How can I understand unless someone guides me?" Consider this book your guide, but remember that your ultimate teacher is the Holy Spirit, who "searcheth all things, yea, the deep things of God" (1 Corinthians 2:10).

You're not as lost as you think. In fact, you might be exactly where God wants you to be—ready to learn, humble enough to admit you need help, and hungry enough to keep going.

Let's begin.

I

Getting Your Bearings

Chapter 1: What Exactly IS the Bible?

Before we dive into how to study the Bible, we need to answer a fundamental question that many people feel embarrassed to ask: What exactly is the Bible? I know it sounds basic, but you'd be surprised how many Christians have been reading Scripture for years without really understanding what they're holding in their hands.

Think of it this way: if someone handed you a phone and told you to use it, you could figure out how to make calls eventually. But if you understood it was also a camera, computer, GPS, and entertainment system, you'd get so much more out of it. The same principle applies to the Bible. The more you understand what it is, the better equipped you'll be to study it effectively.

More Than Just a Religious Book

Let's start with what the Bible is not. It's not a single book written by one person at one time. It's not a collection of nice moral stories. It's not an ancient version of a self-help manual. And it's certainly not a boring religious textbook that only pastors are supposed to understand.

So what is it?

The Bible is God's written revelation of Himself to humanity—His love letter to the world, if you will. It's the primary way God has chosen to communicate who He is, what He's done, and what He expects from us. Peter reminds us, "For the prophecy came not in old time by the will of man: but holy men of God spake as they were moved by the Holy Ghost" (2 Peter 1:21).

This is what theologians call "inspiration," but don't let that fancy word intimidate you. It simply means that while human authors wrote the words using their own personalities, experiences, and writing styles, God guided the process to ensure His message came through clearly and accurately.

A Library, Not a Single Volume

Here's something that might surprise you: the word "Bible" comes from the Greek word "biblios," which means "books"—plural. What we call "the Bible" is a collection of 66 books written by approximately 40 different writers over a period of about 1,500 years. When you think about it that way, it's pretty remarkable that it tells one unified story.

Imagine if 40 people who had never met each other, living in different countries and centuries, all contributed chapters to a novel. You'd expect chaos, right? But the Bible presents a coherent narrative from beginning to end because it has one ultimate Author—God Himself.

These 66 books are divided into two main sections: the Old Testament and the New Testament. The word "testament" simply means "covenant" or "agreement." The Old Testament contains 39 books that tell the story of God's relationship with humanity from creation through about 400 years before Jesus was born. The New Testament contains 27 books that focus on Jesus Christ and the early church.

The Old Testament: God's Covenant with Israel

The Old Testament isn't just ancient history that we can safely ignore now that Jesus has come. Jesus Himself said, "Think not that I am come to destroy the law, or the prophets: I am not come to destroy, but to fulfil" (Matthew 5:17). The Old Testament sets the stage for everything that happens in the New Testament. The Old Testament can be divided into several categories:

The Law (Genesis through Deuteronomy): These first five books, sometimes called the Pentateuch or Torah, contain the foundational stories of creation, the fall, the flood, and God's covenant with Abraham, Isaac, Jacob, and Moses. They also contain the laws God gave to Israel, including the Ten Commandments.

Historical Books (Joshua through Esther): These books tell the story of Israel from their conquest of the Promised Land through their exile and return. Don't worry—you don't need to memorize all the kings and battles. Focus on seeing how God remained faithful to His people even when they were unfaithful to Him.

Poetry and Wisdom Literature (Job through Song of Solomon): This includes books like Psalms (ancient hymns and prayers), Proverbs (practical wisdom for daily living), and Ecclesiastes (deep thoughts about life's meaning). These books teach us how to worship, pray, and live wisely.

Major Prophets (Isaiah through Daniel): These books contain messages from God delivered through His prophets to call His people back to faithfulness. They're called "major" not because they're more important but because they're longer.

Minor Prophets (Hosea through Malachi): Twelve shorter prophetic books that continue the theme of calling God's people to repentance and faithfulness while promising future hope.

The New Testament: God's Covenant Through Christ

The New Testament picks up the story about 400 years after the Old Testament ends. This is where we meet Jesus Christ, the fulfillment of all the Old Testament promises and prophecies.

The Gospels (Matthew, Mark, Luke, John) are four different accounts of Jesus' life, death, and resurrection. Each writer had a different audience and emphasized different aspects of Jesus' ministry, but together, they give us a complete picture of who Jesus is and what He accomplished.

Acts: The historical account of the early church and how the gospel spread from Jerusalem to the rest of the known world. Think of it as "The Adventures of the Apostles."

Paul's Letters (Romans through Philemon): Thirteen letters written by the apostle Paul to various churches and individuals. These letters address practical problems in early churches and explain Christian doctrine in ways we can still apply today.

General Letters (Hebrews through Jude): Eight letters written by various apostles to encourage and instruct believers. They address issues such as perseverance in the face of trials, practical Christian living, and false teaching.

Revelation: A prophetic book that uses symbolic language to describe the ultimate victory of Jesus Christ and God's people. Don't let it intimidate you—its central message is simple: Jesus wins, and those who belong to Him will share in His victory.

One Story, Many Writers, One Author

Despite being written by so many different people over such an extended period, the Bible tells one continuous story. It's the story of God's plan to redeem humanity from the consequences of sin and restore the relationship that was broken in the Garden of Eden.

The Old Testament shows us our need for a Savior. It demonstrates through story after story that human beings, no matter how hard they try, cannot save themselves or maintain a perfect relationship with a holy God. Every hero of the Old Testament—Abraham, Moses, David, and Solomon—had significant flaws and failures.

The New Testament reveals God's solution: Jesus Christ. As John wrote, "For God so loved the world, that he gave his only begotten Son, that whosoever believeth in him should not perish, but have everlasting life" (John 3:16).

This unified message is one of the strongest pieces of evidence of the Bible's divine inspiration. How else could you explain such consistency across so many centuries and cultures?

How We Got the Bible in Our Hands

You might wonder how we can be confident that the Bible we read today is the same as what was originally written. After all, we don't have the original manuscripts that Moses, David, or Paul wrote by hand.

Here's the short answer: we have more ancient manuscript evidence for the Bible than any other ancient document, and the copying process was incredibly careful and precise. The Jewish scribes who copied the Old Testament had elaborate systems to ensure accuracy, counting every letter and even noting each book's middle letter to verify their exact copies.

We have thousands of ancient Greek manuscripts for the New Testament, some dating back to within a few decades of when the originals were written. When scholars compare these manuscripts, they find remarkable consistency. The few minor variations (mostly differences in spelling or word order) don't affect any major biblical doctrine.

Translation: Bringing God's Word to Every Language

Unless you read ancient Hebrew and Greek (and don't worry, most pastors don't either), you're reading a translation of the Bible. This raises an important question: how do we know we can trust our English translations?

The original Old Testament was written primarily in Hebrew, with a few sections in Aramaic. The New Testament was written in Greek—not the classical Greek of philosophers, but the common Greek that ordinary people spoke in the marketplace.

Different translations have different approaches. Some, like the King

James Version, try to stay as close as possible to the original language structure, even when it sounds formal or archaic in English. Others, like the New International Version, aim for thought-for-thought translation that attempts to capture contemporary English's meaning. We'll talk more about choosing a translation in the next chapter.

The key point is this: God wants His Word to be understood by ordinary people in every language. As Isaiah wrote, "So shall my word be that goeth forth out of my mouth: it shall not return unto me void, but it shall accomplish that which I please, and it shall prosper in the thing whereto I sent it" (Isaiah 55:11).

The Bible's Central Theme: Redemption

What would you say if someone asked you to summarize the entire Bible in one sentence? Here's how I'd put it: The Bible is the story of God's plan to redeem fallen humanity through Jesus Christ.

Every story, law, prophecy, and psalm ultimately points to this central theme. Adam and Eve's disobedience in the garden created a problem that only God could solve. The sacrificial system in the Old Testament pointed forward to the ultimate sacrifice of Christ. The promises to Abraham found their fulfillment in Jesus. The kingdom promised to David became a reality when Jesus rose from the dead and ascended to the throne of heaven.

This doesn't mean every verse is directly about Jesus, but it does mean that every part of Scripture contributes to this overarching narrative of redemption. When Jesus walked with the disciples on the road to Emmaus after His resurrection, "beginning at Moses and all the prophets, he expounded unto them in all the scriptures the things concerning himself" (Luke 24:27).

Why This Matters for Bible Study

Understanding what the Bible is fundamentally changes how you approach studying it. You're not just reading ancient literature or collecting moral principles; you're engaging with God's own words about His plan for your life and the world.

This means Bible study is both a privilege and a responsibility. It's a privilege because the Creator of the universe has chosen to reveal Himself to you personally through His Word. It's a responsibility because "unto whomsoever much is given, of him shall be much required" (Luke 12:48).

But don't let the responsibility part scare you. God doesn't expect you to understand everything immediately. He's as patient with our learning process as any good teacher would be. The Ethiopian eunuch we mentioned in the introduction wasn't embarrassed that he needed help understanding Isaiah—he was eager to learn.

Getting Started with Confidence

Now that you understand what the Bible is—God's unified revelation of His redemption plan written through human authors over many centuries—you can approach it with both reverence and confidence.

Reverence, because you're handling the very words of God. As the psalmist wrote, "Thy word is very pure: therefore thy servant loveth it" (Psalm 119:140).

Confidence, because God wants you to understand His Word. He didn't give it to you as a puzzle to solve or a riddle to decode. He gave it to you as a lamp for your path and a light for your feet (Psalm 119:105).

In our next chapter, we'll discuss the practical preparations you must make before opening your Bible. But for now, take a moment to thank God for the incredible gift of His written Word. Forty authors, sixteen centuries, three languages, and one unified message of hope—all preserved and translated so that you can know the God who loves you.

That's not just remarkable—it's miraculous. And it's yours to discover.

Study Questions for Chapter 1:

1. Why is it important to understand what the Bible actually is before learning how to study it effectively? How might misconceptions about the Bible's nature hinder your ability to study it well?

2. What does it mean that the Bible is "God's written revelation of Himself to humanity" rather than just a collection of religious writings? How should this understanding affect your approach to Bible study?

3. The chapter explains that 40 different authors wrote the Bible's 66 books over 1,500 years, yet it tells one unified story. What does this suggest about the Bible's ultimate Author, and how does this impact your confidence in Scripture's reliability?

4. How do the Old Testament and New Testament work together to reveal God's plan of redemption? Give an example of how an Old Testament passage points forward to something fulfilled in the New Testament.

5. What is the central theme that runs throughout all of Scripture, and how does recognizing this theme help you understand individual passages better?

Practice Exercise: Take a "Bible tour" by reading one chapter from each major section: Genesis 1 (Law), Joshua 1 (History), Psalm 23 (Poetry), Isaiah 53 (Prophecy), John 3 (Gospels), and Romans 8 (Epistles). For each passage, write down: (1) what it teaches about God's character, (2) what it reveals about humanity, and (3) how it connects to the central theme of redemption through Christ. Notice how these diverse passages from different authors and time periods all contribute to the same overarching story of God's love and salvation.

Chapter 2: Before You Even Open the Book

You wouldn't start building a house without the right tools, and you shouldn't start studying the Bible without proper preparation. But here's the good news: you need far fewer tools than you might think, and most of what you need is probably already within your reach.

Before discussing study methods and techniques, we need to address some basic questions: Which Bible should you use? What tools do you actually need? How should you set up your study time and space? These might seem like simple questions, but getting them right will make all the difference in your Bible study journey.

Choosing Your Bible Translation: Why the King James Version Stands Apart

Walk into any Christian bookstore, and you'll be overwhelmed by the number of Bible translations available. The New International Version, the English Standard Version, the New Living Translation, the Message—the options seem endless. With so many choices, how do you know which one to use?

Let me make a case for starting with the King James Version, and I hope you'll hear me out even if you've heard arguments against it.

The King James Version, first published in 1611, has been the standard English Bible for over 400 years. That longevity isn't accidental—it's a testament to its accuracy and enduring power to communicate God's Word effectively. When you read the KJV, you're reading the same translation that strengthened the faith of countless believers through centuries of persecution, revival, and spiritual growth.

The Foundation of Manuscript Evidence

The King James Version is based on what scholars call the Textus Receptus, or "Received Text," the collection of Greek manuscripts that the early church recognized and preserved as authentic Scripture. These manuscripts were copied and recopied by believers who treasured God's Word and took extraordinary care to maintain it accurately.

Modern translations rely heavily on manuscripts discovered in the 19th and 20th centuries, particularly Codex Sinaiticus and Codex Vaticanus. While these manuscripts are certainly ancient, they were found in unusual circumstances—Sinaiticus was literally found in a monastery trash bin, and Vaticanus was hidden away in the Vatican library for centuries. The question we should ask is this: Why weren't these manuscripts being used and copied by the early church if they were considered reliable?

On the other hand, the manuscripts underlying the King James Version were worn out from use. They had to be copied again and again because believers were constantly reading, studying, and sharing them. This is exactly what you'd expect to happen to authentic Scripture—it would be treasured, used, and carefully preserved by God's people.

The Precision of Translation

The King James translators were not just scholars; they were men who feared God and approached His Word with reverence. They worked in groups, checking each other's work, and they understood that they were handling the very words of the Almighty. Their goal wasn't to make the Bible sound contemporary or easy to read but to accurately convey what God had said.

Modern translations often prioritize readability over precision, which can lead to significant changes in meaning. For example, many newer translations change "repent" to "turn from your sins," but these aren't the same. Repentance (from the Greek "metanoia") means a change of mind that leads to a change of direction. Adding the concept of turning from sins changes the emphasis and can lead to confusion about salvation by grace through faith.

The KJV translators carefully distinguished between Greek and Hebrew words, even when English doesn't have perfect equivalents. This precision might make some passages more challenging to read, but it also preserves important theological distinctions lost in simplified translations.

The Beauty and Power of Language

There's something to be said for the majesty and dignity of King James English. When the Bible speaks of God's holiness, judgment, and mercy, the KJV's formal language matches the subject matter's weight. Compare these two renderings of Isaiah 6:3:

KJV: "And one cried unto another, and said, Holy, holy, holy, is the LORD of hosts: the whole earth is full of his glory."

NIV: "And they were calling to one another: 'Holy, holy, holy is the LORD Almighty; the whole earth is full of his glory.'"

Both are accurate, but the KJV conveys a sense of awe and reverence that matches the scene of heavenly worship. The language itself reminds us that we're not reading ordinary literature—we're encountering the words of the eternal God.

Addressing Common Concerns

"But the language is too hard to understand!" I hear this objection frequently, and I understand it. Some of the language in the KJV is archaic. But here's what I've discovered in over twenty years of teaching: people who struggle with KJV language usually struggle with Bible content, not just Bible language. The concepts of sin, redemption, sanctification, and eternal judgment are profound regardless of which translation you use.

Moreover, wrestling with slightly challenging language can strengthen your understanding. When you have to think carefully about what a passage means, you're more likely to remember it and apply it to your life.

"What about all those 'thee's and 'thou's?" These archaic pronouns serve an important purpose. In the original Greek and Hebrew, there's a distinction between singular and plural forms of "you." English has lost this distinction, but the KJV preserves it by using "thee" and "thou" for singular and "ye" and "you" for plural. This distinction can help clarify whether a passage is addressing an individual or a group, sometimes a crucial distinction for proper interpretation.

The Italicized Words: A Translator's Tool for Transparency

One of the most distinctive features of the King James Version is its use of italicized words, and understanding their purpose will help you study more effectively. If you've ever wondered why certain words appear in italics in your KJV, you're asking exactly the right question.

What the Italics Mean

The italicized words in the KJV are words that the translators added to make the English readable but don't have direct equivalents in the original Hebrew or Greek texts. This wasn't done carelessly or to change the meaning—quite the opposite. The translators wanted to be completely transparent about what they were doing.

For example, in Genesis 1:16, the KJV reads: "And God made two great lights; the greater light to rule the day, and the lesser light to rule the night: *he made* the stars also." The words "he made" are in italics because they don't appear in the Hebrew text but are necessary for the sentence to make sense in English.

Why This Matters for Bible Study

Understanding italicized words can actually enhance your Bible study in several ways:

They show you the translator's interpretation. When you see italicized words, you see how the translators understood the passage. This understanding can help you think more carefully about alternative ways to understand the text.

They highlight the differences between languages. Hebrew and Greek don't always structure sentences the same way English does. The italicized words show where the translators had to add something to make the translation readable.

They encourage careful reading. When you notice italicized words, they prompt you to think more carefully about what the original text might have said and how you might understand it.

Examples of Helpful Italics

Consider Romans 1:17: "For therein is the righteousness of God revealed from faith to faith: as it is written, The just shall live *by* faith." The word "by" is italicized because the Greek text simply says, "The just shall live faith." The translators added "by" to clarify the relationship, but knowing that it's not in the original text helps you understand that faith is emphasized as the means of spiritual life.

In 1 Corinthians 10:24, we read: "Let no man seek his own, but every man another's *wealth*." The word "wealth" is italicized because the Greek text just says "another's." The translators added "wealth" to complete the thought, but you could just as easily understand it as "another's good" or "another's benefit." Seeing the italics helps you understand the broader principle rather than getting locked into one specific interpretation.

Essential Tools You Actually Need

Now that we've settled on using the King James Version as your primary Bible, let's talk about what other tools you need. The answer might surprise you: not many.

A Good Study Bible

A study Bible includes notes, cross-references, maps, and other helps printed alongside the biblical text. I recommend the Scofield Reference Bible or the Thompson Chain Reference Bible for KJV readers. These study Bibles have helped millions of Christians understand Scripture better without overwhelming them with too much information.

The notes in a good study Bible can help explain historical context, define difficult terms, and point you to related passages. But remember: the notes are helpful commentary, not inspired Scripture. Always let the Bible interpret itself before consulting human explanations.

A Concordance

A concordance is an alphabetical index of words used in the Bible, showing you every verse where each word appears. The Strong's Exhaustive Concordance is the gold standard for KJV users. It lists every occurrence of every word and provides the original Hebrew or Greek word behind each English translation.

For example, if you want to study what the Bible says about "love," a concordance will show you every verse that uses that word. Strong's will also show you that sometimes "love" translates the Greek word "agape" (sacrificial love) and sometimes "phileo" (friendship love), helping you understand the different nuances.

A Bible Dictionary

A good Bible dictionary explains people, places, customs, and concepts mentioned in Scripture. It can help you understand who the Pharisees were, what a phylactery was, or why certain animals were considered unclean. Easton's Bible Dictionary or Smith's Bible Dictionary are excellent choices that complement the KJV well.

What You Don't Need (Yet)

You don't need a library of commentaries to get started. You don't need software that analyzes Greek and Hebrew for you. You don't need study guides that break down every chapter into discussion questions. These tools can be helpful later, but they can also become crutches that keep you from learning to study the Bible for yourself.

The most important tool you need is one you already have: the Holy Spirit. Jesus promised His disciples, "But the Comforter, which is the Holy Ghost, whom the Father will send in my name, he shall teach you all things, and bring all things to your remembrance, whatsoever I have said unto you" (John 14:26).

Setting Up Your Study Space And Habit

Your physical environment affects your ability to concentrate and learn. You don't need a fancy home office or a library, but you need a space where you can focus without constant interruption.

Find Your Quiet Place

Jesus said, "But thou, when thou prayest, enter into thy closet, and when thou hast shut thy door, pray to thy Father which is in secret; and thy Father which seeth in secret shall reward thee openly" (Matthew 6:6). While this verse is specifically about prayer, the principle applies to Bible study as well. You need a place where you can shut out distractions and focus on God's Word.

This place might be a corner of your bedroom, a spot at your kitchen table early in the morning, or even your car during lunch break. The location matters less than the consistency and freedom from interruption.

Keep It Simple

You need a comfortable place to sit, good lighting, space for your Bible, and perhaps a notebook. That's it. Don't let the lack of a perfect study setup keep you from getting started.

Setting Up Your Study Time

When you study matters almost as much as how you study. Most people find that consistency is more important than duration—fifteen minutes every day will accomplish more than two hours once a week.

Morning, Evening, or Anytime?

David wrote, "My voice shalt thou hear in the morning, O LORD; in the morning will I direct my prayer unto thee, and will look up" (Psalm 5:3). There's something special about starting your day with God's Word before the pressures and distractions of daily life take over.

But not everyone is a morning person, and that's okay. The key is finding a time when you're alert and unlikely to be interrupted. Some study during lunch breaks, others in the evening after the children are in bed. Find what works for your schedule and stick with it.

Start Small and Build

If you've never had a regular Bible study habit, don't start by trying to study for an hour every day. Begin with ten or fifteen minutes and gradually increase as the habit becomes established. It's better to study consistently for a short time than to burn out trying to do too much too soon.

The Most Important Preparation: Prayer

Before you open your Bible, open your heart to God in prayer. The psalmist prayed, "Open thou mine eyes, that I may behold wondrous things out of thy law" (Psalm 119:18). This should be your prayer too.

Ask God to help you understand what you're reading, show you how to apply it to your life, and protect you from pride or presumption as you study His Word. The Bible is unlike any other book because it has a divine Author who wants to speak to you personally through its pages.

Realistic Expectations for Beginners

As you begin this journey, it's essential to have realistic expectations. You won't understand everything you read, and that's okay. You won't have profound insights every time you study, and that's normal. Some days will feel more productive, and some passages will seem more relevant to your life than others.

You can expect gradual growth in understanding and application. As Isaiah wrote, "For precept must be upon precept, precept upon precept; line upon line, line upon line; here a little, and there a little" (Isaiah 28:10). Bible study is a process of gradual building, not instant illumination.

You can also expect God to honor your sincere effort to know Him through His Word. He promises, "And ye shall seek me, and find me, when ye shall search for me with all your heart" (Jeremiah 29:13).

Ready to Begin

You now have everything you need to begin studying God's Word effectively: a reliable translation (the KJV), basic tools to help you understand what you're reading, a plan for when and where to study, and realistic expectations for the journey ahead.

In our next chapter, we'll look at the big picture of Scripture—the overarching story that ties all 66 books of the Bible together. Understanding this framework will help you see how individual passages fit into God's grand plan of redemption.

But first, take a moment to prepare your heart. Pray the psalmist's prayer: "Teach me, O LORD, the way of thy statutes; and I shall keep it unto the end. Give me understanding, and I shall keep thy law; yea, I shall observe it with my whole heart" (Psalm 119:33-34).

God is ready to meet with you in His Word. Are you ready to meet with Him?

Study Questions for Chapter 2:

1. Why does this chapter recommend the King James Version as your primary study Bible? What are the key arguments presented for the KJV's reliability and usefulness for serious Bible study?

2. How do the italicized words in the KJV help you understand the translation process? Give an example of how recognizing italicized words might affect your interpretation of a passage.

3. What is the difference between starting with expensive study resources versus beginning with basic, essential tools? Why does the chapter emphasize that you need fewer tools than you might think to study effectively?

4. How does your physical study environment affect your ability to

MAKING THE BIBLE CLEAR

concentrate and maintain consistent Bible study habits? What changes could you make to create a better study space?

5. What role should prayer play in preparing for Bible study? How does approaching Scripture with the right heart attitude affect your ability to understand and apply God's Word?

Practice Exercise: Set up your personal Bible study space using the guidelines from this chapter. Gather your essential tools (KJV Bible, notebook, pen), choose a consistent location with minimal distractions, and establish a specific time for study. For one week, spend 15 minutes each day reading through Psalm 119:1-48, paying special attention to any italicized words in your KJV and noting what the psalmist says about God's Word. Begin each session with the prayer from Psalm 119:18: "Open thou mine eyes, that I may behold wondrous things out of thy law." Keep a simple journal of what you observe and how your study environment affects your concentration and enjoyment.

Chapter 3: The Big Picture First

Imagine trying to put together a 1,000-piece jigsaw puzzle without the picture on the box to guide you. You might get a few pieces to fit together here and there, but you'd quickly become frustrated because you wouldn't know what you were building toward. Many Christians approach Bible study the same way—they jump into individual verses or stories without understanding how they fit into the larger picture.

That's what this chapter is designed to prevent. Before we dive into specific study methods, we need to take a step back and see the forest before examining the trees. The Bible tells one magnificent, unified story from Genesis to Revelation, and understanding that story will transform how you read every individual passage.

The Bible's Grand Narrative: God's Plan of Redemption

If I had to summarize the entire Bible in one sentence, here's what I'd say: The Bible is the story of God creating a perfect world, humanity's rebellion that broke that perfection, and God's gracious plan to restore everything through Jesus Christ.

This isn't just my summary—it's woven throughout Scripture itself. Jesus told His disciples after His resurrection, "And he said unto them, These are the words which I spake unto you, while I was yet with you, that all things must be fulfilled, which were written in the law of Moses, and in the prophets, and in the psalms, concerning me" (Luke 24:44). The entire Old Testament points forward to Christ, and the New Testament reveals Him as the fulfillment of all God's promises.

Let's trace this grand story through its major movements.

Act I: Creation and the Perfect Beginning (Genesis 1-2)

The Bible begins not with philosophy or abstract theology but with action: "In the beginning God created the heaven and the earth" (Genesis 1:1). These opening words establish several crucial truths that echo throughout the rest of Scripture.

First, God exists before and outside of His creation. He isn't part of the natural world—He made it. This means He has authority over it and the right to establish its laws and purposes.

Second, God creates by speaking. "And God said, Let there be light: and there was light" (Genesis 1:3). Throughout Scripture, God's word is presented as powerful and effective. When God speaks, things happen. This should give us confidence as we study His written Word—it isn't just human literature but the powerful word of the same God who spoke the universe into existence.

Third, God's creation is good. After each day of creation, "God saw that it was good," and after creating mankind, "God saw every thing that he had made, and, behold, it was very good" (Genesis 1:31). This original goodness is important because it shows us that the problems we see in the world today—death, disease, natural disasters, human cruelty—aren't part of God's original design.

The pinnacle of God's creation was humanity: "And God said, Let us make man in our image, after our likeness... So God created man in his own image, in the image of God created he him; male and female created he them" (Genesis 1:26-27). Being made in God's image means human beings have inherent dignity, worth, and purpose. We were created for a relationship with God and with each other.

In the Garden of Eden, we see God's original intention for humanity: perfect fellowship with our Creator, harmony in human relationships, meaningful work without frustration, and life without death. Adam and Eve walked with God "in the cool of the day" (Genesis 3:8), experiencing the kind of relationship with their Creator that every human heart still longs for.

Act II: The Fall and the Problem of Sin (Genesis 3-11)

But this perfect beginning didn't last. Genesis 3 records the tragic account of humanity's rebellion against God. God had given Adam and Eve freedom to enjoy everything in the garden except one tree: "But of the tree of the knowledge of good and evil, thou shalt not eat of it: for in the day that thou eatest thereof thou shalt surely die" (Genesis 2:17).

This wasn't an arbitrary restriction. God was essentially saying, "I am God, and you are not. Trust me to determine what is good and evil rather than deciding for yourselves." The forbidden tree represented the fundamental choice every human faces: Will we submit to God's authority, or will we try to be our own gods?

When Adam and Eve chose to eat from the forbidden tree, they weren't just breaking a rule—they were declaring their independence from God. The results were immediate and catastrophic. Shame entered their relationship with God, requiring them to hide from His presence. Conflict entered their relationship with each other, as Adam blamed both Eve and God for his own choice: "The woman whom thou gavest to be with me, she gave me of the tree, and I did eat" (Genesis 3:12). Their work became frustrating and challenging. And death entered the human experience.

Most importantly, their relationship with God was broken. They could no longer walk with Him in the cool of the day. They were kicked out of the garden and barred from the Tree of Life.

But even in this moment of judgment, God showed mercy. He promised that One would come who would defeat the serpent who had tempted them: "And I will put enmity between thee and the woman, and between thy seed and her seed; it shall bruise thy head, and thou shalt bruise his heel" (Genesis 3:15). This is the first messianic promise in Scripture—the first hint of God's plan to solve the problem that sin had created.

The following chapters of Genesis illustrate the devastating effects of sin spreading throughout humanity. Cain murdered his brother Abel. Violence increased until God had to judge the world with a flood, saving only Noah and his family. Even after the Flood, human pride led to the Tower of Babel, where people attempted to make themselves equal to God. The pattern is clear: humanity cannot solve its problem of sin. We need a Savior.

Act III: God Chooses a People (Genesis 12 - Malachi)

Rather than abandoning His rebellious creation, God chose to work through one man and his descendants to bring salvation to the world. He called Abraham (originally named Abram) with this promise: "Now the LORD had said unto Abram, Get thee out of thy country, and from thy kindred, and from thy father's house, unto a land that I will shew thee: And I will make of thee a great nation, and I will bless thee, and make thy name great; and thou shalt be a blessing: And I will bless them that bless thee, and curse him that curseth thee: and in thee shall all families of the earth be blessed" (Genesis 12:1-3).

Notice that last phrase: "in thee shall all families of the earth be blessed." From the very beginning, God's plan wasn't just to save one nation but to bring salvation to the entire world through Abraham's descendants.

The Patriarchs: God's Promises Take Root

God renewed His covenant promises with Abraham's son Isaac and grandson Jacob (later renamed Israel). These men weren't perfect—they made serious mistakes and had significant character flaws. But God remained faithful to His promises despite their failures, demonstrating that His plan of salvation relies on His faithfulness, not human perfection.

The Exodus: God Delivers His People

The descendants of Abraham, Isaac, and Jacob ended up as slaves in Egypt for 400 years, just as God had predicted. But in God's timing, He raised up Moses to deliver them. The exodus from Egypt is one of the most significant events in the Old Testament, as it demonstrates God's power to save and His faithfulness in keeping His promises.

The Passover lamb, whose blood protected the Israelites from God's judgment on Egypt, points forward to Jesus Christ, "the Lamb of God, which taketh away the sin of the world" (John 1:29). The crossing of the Red Sea pictures the salvation that delivers us from the power of sin.

At Mount Sinai, God gave the Law through Moses. This wasn't God's attempt to provide a way for people to earn salvation through good works. Instead, the Law served several purposes: it revealed God's holy character, demonstrated the seriousness of sin, and pointed forward to the need for a perfect sacrifice for sin.

The Promised Land and the Kingdom

After 40 years in the wilderness, God brought the Israelites into the Promised Land under Joshua's leadership. But even in the land of promise, the people continued to struggle with sin and rebellion. The book of Judges shows a repeated cycle: the people would turn away from God, experience the consequences of their sin, cry out to God for help, and be delivered by a judge whom God raised up.

Eventually, the people demanded a king "like all the nations" (1 Samuel 8:5). God gave them what they wanted, first Saul, then David. David was "a man after God's own heart" (1 Samuel 13:14), not because he was sinless, but because he genuinely repented when he sinned and trusted in God's mercy.

God promised David that his kingdom would be eternal: "And thine house and thy kingdom shall be established for ever before thee: thy throne shall be established for ever" (2 Samuel 7:16). This promise finds its ultimate fulfillment in Jesus Christ, who is called "the son of David" throughout the New Testament.

The Prophets: Calling People Back to God

After David's son Solomon, the kingdom was divided into two parts: Israel (the northern kingdom) and Judah (the southern kingdom). Both kingdoms struggled with idolatry, injustice, and unfaithfulness to God's covenant.

God raised up prophets to call His people back to faithfulness and to warn them of the consequences of continued rebellion. But the prophets didn't just bring messages of judgment—they also brought hope. They spoke of a coming Messiah who would establish God's kingdom perfectly and permanently.

Isaiah spoke of a virgin who would conceive and bear a son called "Immanuel" (Isaiah 7:14). He described a suffering servant who would "bear our griefs, and carry our sorrows" and be "wounded for our transgressions" (Isaiah 53:4-5). Micah predicted that the Messiah would be born in Bethlehem (Micah 5:2). Daniel spoke of one "like the Son of man" who would receive an everlasting kingdom (Daniel 7:13-14).

The Exile and Return: Judgment and Hope

Due to continued unfaithfulness, both kingdoms were eventually conquered and taken into exile—Israel by the Assyrians in 722 BC and Judah by the Babylonians in 586 BC. The temple in Jerusalem was destroyed, and it seemed like God's promises had failed.

But God remained faithful even in judgment. He brought a remnant of His people back to the land after 70 years in Babylon, and they rebuilt the temple and the walls of Jerusalem under leaders like Ezra and Nehemiah.

However, the return from exile didn't solve the fundamental problem of sin. The people continued to struggle with the same issues that had led to exile in the first place. The Old Testament concludes with Malachi's prophecy, promising that God would send "Elijah the prophet before the coming of the great and dreadful day of the LORD" (Malachi 4:5).

Act IV: The Coming of the King (Matthew - John)

After 400 years of silence, God spoke again. An angel appeared to a young virgin named Mary with an announcement that would change the world: "And the angel said unto her, Fear not, Mary: for thou hast found favour with God. And, behold, thou shalt conceive in thy womb, and bring forth a son, and shalt call his name JESUS. He shall be great, and shall be called the Son of the Highest: and the Lord God shall give unto him the throne of his father David" (Luke 1:30-32).

Jesus Christ is the fulfillment of every Old Testament promise and prophecy. He is the seed of the woman who would crush the serpent's head. He is the offspring of Abraham through whom all nations would be blessed. He is the prophet like Moses, whom God promised to raise up. He is the son of David, whose kingdom would be eternal. He is the suffering servant of Isaiah who would bear our sins.

The Perfect Life

Where Adam failed in a perfect garden, Jesus succeeded in a fallen world. He lived the perfect life that God required but that no human being had ever lived. "For he hath made him to be sin for us, who knew no sin; that we might be made the righteousness of God in him" (2 Corinthians 5:21).

Jesus demonstrated His deity through His miracles, His teachings, and His authority over creation, demons, and death itself. But He also showed His true humanity by experiencing hunger, thirst, fatigue, and all the other limitations of human life—except sin.

The Perfect Sacrifice

The ceremonial sacrifices of the Old Testament could never actually take away sin—they were temporary coverings that pointed forward to the ultimate sacrifice to come. As the writer of Hebrews explains, "For it is not possible that the blood of bulls and of goats should take away sins" (Hebrews 10:4).

But when Jesus died on the cross, He offered the perfect sacrifice for sin once and for all. "But this man, after he had offered one sacrifice for sins for ever, sat down on the right hand of God" (Hebrews 10:12). His death satisfied God's justice and made it possible for God to forgive sinners without compromising His holiness.

The Victory Over Death

Jesus' resurrection from the dead proved that the Father accepted His sacrifice and that death—the consequence of sin—had been defeated. "But now is Christ risen from the dead, and become the firstfruits of them that slept" (1 Corinthians 15:20).

Act V: The Church and the Great Commission (Acts - Revelation)

Before ascending to heaven, Jesus gave His disciples the Great Commission: "Go ye therefore, and teach all nations, baptizing them in the name of the Father, and of the Son, and of the Holy Ghost: Teaching them to observe all things whatsoever I have commanded you: and, lo, I am with you alway, even unto the end of the world" (Matthew 28:19-20).

The Book of Acts records how the early church carried out this commission, beginning in Jerusalem and spreading throughout the Roman Empire. The gospel went first to the Jews, then to the Samaritans, and finally to the Gentiles, fulfilling God's promise to Abraham that all nations would be blessed through his offspring.

The epistles (letters) in the New Testament were written to explain the implications of Christ's work and to help believers understand how to live in light of the gospel. They address practical questions about Christian living, church organization, and doctrinal issues that arose in the early churches.

Act VI: The Final Victory (Revelation)

The Bible ends where it began—with God in complete control, and His creation restored to perfection. The book of Revelation, despite its challenging symbolic language, has a simple message: Jesus wins.

John saw "a new heaven and a new earth: for the first heaven and the first earth were passed away" (Revelation 21:1). He heard a voice from heaven saying, "Behold, the tabernacle of God is with men, and he will dwell with them, and they shall be his people, and God himself shall be with them, and be their God. And God shall wipe away all tears from their eyes; and there shall be no more death, neither sorrow, nor crying, neither shall there be any more pain: for the former things are passed away" (Revelation 21:3-4).

This is the ultimate fulfillment of God's plan of redemption—perfect fellowship between God and His people restored, sin and its consequences eliminated forever, and the original purpose of creation finally achieved.

Key Themes That Run Throughout Scripture

Understanding the Bible's overarching story helps us recognize several key themes that appear throughout Scripture:

Covenant

God is a covenant-making God who binds Himself by promises to His people. From His covenant with Noah after the Flood to the new covenant established through Christ's blood, God consistently demonstrates His faithfulness to His promises, even when His people are unfaithful.

Sacrifice

From the coats of skins that God made to clothe Adam and Eve to the Lamb's book of life in Revelation, the Bible consistently teaches that sin requires a blood sacrifice. The Old Testament sacrifices all pointed forward to Christ's ultimate sacrifice on the cross.

Kingdom

God is King, and His kingdom is the central theme of Jesus' teaching. The kingdom was promised to David, proclaimed by the prophets, inaugurated by Jesus, and will be fully established when He returns.

Redemption

God is in the business of buying back what was lost. He redeemed Israel from slavery in Egypt, He redeems individuals from slavery to sin, and He will ultimately redeem all of creation from the curse of sin.

Why the Big Picture Matters for Bible Study

Understanding this overarching narrative will transform how you read individual passages:

It prevents misinterpretation. When you understand how a passage fits into the larger story, you're less likely to take it out of context or misapply it.

It increases your appreciation. Seeing how Old Testament stories point forward to Christ makes them more meaningful and relevant.

It builds your confidence. Understanding the Bible's unified message helps you recognize that apparent contradictions often arise from a lack of understanding of how different passages relate to the overall narrative.

It guides your application. Knowing where we are in God's plan of redemption helps you apply biblical principles appropriately to your current situation.

Major Characters You'll Encounter

As you read through Scripture, you'll meet many people who play essential roles in God's plan of redemption. Here are some key figures to watch for:

Adam - the first man, whose disobedience brought sin into the world; **Abraham** - the father of faith, through whom God promised to bless all nations; **Moses** - the lawgiver and deliverer who led Israel out of Egypt; **David** - the King after God's own heart, to whom God promised an eternal kingdom; **The Prophets** - men like Isaiah, Jeremiah, and Daniel who spoke God's word to His people; **John the Baptist** - the forerunner who prepared the way for Jesus; **Jesus Christ** - the Son of God who fulfilled all of God's promises; **Paul** - the apostle to the Gentiles who explained the implications of the gospel; **John** - the beloved disciple who received the revelation of Christ's final victory

A Timeline to Keep in Mind

While you don't need to memorize all the dates, having a general sense of biblical chronology helps put the pieces together:

- **Creation to Abraham** (Genesis 1-11): The beginning of everything and humanity's fall
- **Abraham to Moses** (Genesis 12 - Exodus): God chooses a people (c. 2000-1500 BC)
- **Moses to David** (Exodus - 1 Samuel): The Law, the wilderness, and the conquest (c. 1500-1000 BC)
- **David to the Exile** (2 Samuel - 2 Kings): The kingdom and its division (c. 1000-586 BC)

- **Exile to Christ** (Ezra - Malachi): Return and restoration (586 BC - 4 BC)
- **Christ's Life and Ministry** (Gospels): The fulfillment of all promises (4 BC - 30 AD)
- **The Early Church** (Acts - Revelation): The gospel goes to all nations (30-100 AD)

How the Old Testament Points to Jesus

Now that you understand the big picture, you can see how "all the scriptures" speak of Christ, just as Jesus told His disciples. The Old Testament points to Jesus in several ways:

Through Types and Shadows: The Passover lamb, the bronze serpent, and the temple sacrifices—all picture different aspects of Christ's work.

Through Direct Prophecies: Hundreds of specific predictions about the Messiah's birth, life, death, and resurrection.

Through the Law: The moral law reveals our need for a Savior; the ceremonial law foreshadows the work He would accomplish.

Through History: The pattern of God's faithfulness despite human failure points to the need for a perfect mediator.

Ready for the Details

Now that you understand the forest, you're ready to examine the trees. In our next chapter, we'll learn a simple but powerful method for studying individual passages that will help you see how each piece fits into this magnificent whole.

But before we move on, take a moment to marvel at what God has done. From the moment sin entered the world in Genesis 3, He had a plan to fix what was broken. Every story, every law, every prophecy was part of that plan. And at just the right time, "God sent forth his Son, made of a woman, made under the law, To redeem them that were under the law, that we might receive the adoption of sons" (Galatians 4:4-5).

You're not just reading an ancient book—you're discovering your place in the greatest story ever told.

Study Questions for Chapter 3:

1. Why is it important to understand the "big picture" of Scripture before diving into a detailed study of individual passages? How does knowing the overarching storyline help prevent you from getting lost in details?

2. The chapter describes Scripture as telling one unified story from Creation to New Creation. What are the major themes (like covenant, redemption, and God's faithfulness) that appear throughout this storyline, and how do they connect different parts of the Bible?

3. How does understanding that you're reading about real historical events and real people affect your approach to Bible study? What's the difference between reading biblical narratives as moral lessons versus understanding them as part of God's actual work in history?

4. What does it mean that the Bible shows both God's holiness and His grace throughout the storyline? How do you see both of these attributes working together rather than conflicting with each other?

5. How does seeing the Bible as one continuous story help you understand difficult or confusing passages? Give an example of how a challenging verse might make more sense when you understand its place in the larger narrative.

Practice Exercise: Create your own "Bible storyline timeline" by reading these key passages in order: Genesis 3:15 (the first promise of redemption), Genesis 12:1-3 (God's covenant with Abraham), Exodus 12:1-13 (the Passover), 2 Samuel 7:12-16 (God's promise to David), Isaiah 53:4-6 (prophecy of the suffering Servant), Matthew 1:21 (Jesus' birth announcement), John 19:30 (Jesus' death), and Revelation 21:3-4 (the final restoration). For each passage, write one sentence explaining how it fits into the overarching story of God's plan to redeem humanity. Notice how each passage builds on what came before and points forward to what comes next, showing the unity of God's redemptive plan throughout Scripture.

II

Basic Bible Study Methods That Actually Work

Chapter 4: The LIGHT Method - Your New Best Friend

Do you remember when you first learned to drive? There were so many things to think about—the gas pedal, the brake, checking mirrors, watching for other cars—that you probably felt overwhelmed. But eventually, all those separate actions became second nature, flowing together into the simple act of driving.

Bible study can feel the same way at first. Where do you start? What questions should you ask? How do you move from reading words on a page to understanding what God is saying to you? You need a method that's simple enough to remember but thorough enough to help you dig deep into Scripture.

That's where the LIGHT method comes in. LIGHT stands for Learn, Interpret, Grow, Hear, and Trust. It's a framework that thousands of Christians have used to transform their Bible study from overwhelming confusion into a meaningful encounter with God's Word. The psalmist's declaration inspired the method: "Thy word is a lamp unto my feet, and a light unto my path" (Psalm 119:105).

Why You Need a Method

Before we dive into LIGHT itself, let's address an important question: why do you need a method at all? Can't you just read the Bible and let the Holy Spirit teach you?

Absolutely, the Holy Spirit is your ultimate teacher. Jesus promised, "But the Comforter, which is the Holy Ghost, whom the Father will send in my name, he shall teach you all things, and bring all things to your remembrance, whatsoever I have said unto you" (John 14:26). But having a method doesn't replace the Spirit's work—it creates space for it.

Think of a method like a riverbank. The river (God's truth) is mighty and life-giving, but without banks to guide its flow, it can scatter in all directions and lose its force. A good Bible study method provides a structure that helps you focus your attention and think carefully about what God is saying.

The LIGHT method is beneficial because it prevents two common mistakes beginners make: reading too quickly without really thinking about what they've read and jumping straight to the application without understanding what the passage actually means.

L is for Learn: Read with Purpose

The first step in the LIGHT method is Learn—but this isn't just casual reading. You're reading with purpose, looking for what God wants to say to you through His Word. As Paul wrote to Timothy, "Give attendance to reading" (1 Timothy 4:13).

Choose Your Passage

Start with a manageable portion of Scripture. For beginners, I recommend starting with a single chapter or even just a few verses. It's better to study a small passage thoroughly than to rush through several chapters superficially.

If you're just beginning, consider starting with one of these beginner-friendly books:

- **The Gospel According to John**: Shows Jesus' identity and mission clearly
- **First John**: Practical teaching about Christian living and assurance
- **Philippians**: Paul's joyful letter about contentment and perseverance
- **Psalms**: Choose individual psalms for devotional reading

Read It Multiple Times

Here's where many people miss out on deeper understanding: they read a passage once and move on. Instead, read your chosen passage at least three times before moving to the interpretation stage.

- **First reading**: Get the general idea of what's happening
- **Second reading**: Notice details you missed the first time
- **Third reading**: Look for keywords, repeated phrases, or concepts that stand out

I often tell people to read their chosen passage out loud at least once. There's something about hearing Scripture that helps us catch things our eyes might skip over. Plus, Paul reminds us that "faith cometh by hearing, and hearing by the word of God" (Romans 10:17).

Write Down What It Says

Don't just read—write. Identify key phrases, important words, or verses that stand out to you. Writing down what the passage says helps you slow down and pay attention to details you might otherwise miss.

For example, if you're reading John 3:16, you might write down: "God so loved the world—not just believers, but the whole world. That He gave His only begotten Son. That whosoever believeth in Him shall not perish but have eternal life."

Look for the Main Point

As you read, ask yourself: What is the central message of this passage? If you had to summarize it in one sentence, what would you say? Don't worry about getting this perfect—the goal is to start thinking about the passage's central theme.

For example, when reading John 3:16, the main point is clearly God's love expressed through the giving of His Son for salvation. If you're reading Psalm 23, the main point is God's care and provision for His people.

I is for Interpret: Understand What It Means

Interpretation is where you move from knowing what the passage says to understanding what it means. This step is crucial because you can't properly apply Scripture until you know what it's actually teaching. As Paul urged Timothy, we must be "rightly dividing the word of truth" (2 Timothy 2:15).

Ask the Basic Questions

Start with the fundamental questions that help you understand the passage:

Who? Who is speaking? Who is being addressed? Who are the main characters in the passage? Understanding the people involved helps you understand the context and purpose of the passage.

What? What is happening? What is being said? What actions are taking place? What concepts or ideas are being discussed?

When? When did these events take place? Is this during Jesus' earthly ministry, after His resurrection, or in the Old Testament period? Sometimes, the timing affects the meaning.

Where? Where do these events occur? The location can sometimes be significant for understanding the message.

Why? Why is this being said or done? What prompted this conversation or action? What problem is being addressed?

How? How did these events unfold? How does this passage connect to what comes before and after it?

Consider the Context

Context is king when it comes to interpretation. Always consider:

Immediate context: What comes right before and after this passage? How does it fit into the surrounding verses?

Chapter context: What's the central theme of this chapter, and how does this passage contribute to that theme?

Book context: What was the author's purpose in writing this book, and how does this passage serve that purpose?

Look for Literary Features

The Bible uses various literary techniques to communicate truth, and noticing them will deepen your understanding.

Repetition: When words or phrases are repeated, pay attention. The repetition is intentional and typically emphasizes a key point. For example, in Psalm 136, the phrase "for his mercy endureth for ever" is repeated 26 times—clearly, God wants us to remember His enduring mercy.

Contrasts: Look for words like "but," "however," or "nevertheless" that signals a contrast. These often highlight important distinctions. For instance, Ephesians 2:4 says, "But God, who is rich in mercy..." The word "but" signals a dramatic contrast between our desperate condition and God's gracious response.

Comparisons: Watch for words like "like" or "as" that introduce comparisons. Jesus often used comparisons to help people understand spiritual truths: "The kingdom of heaven is like..."

Questions: When you see questions in Scripture, ask yourself whether they're rhetorical (meant to make a point) or genuine requests for information. Questions often reveal essential truths about human nature or God's character.

Commands and Promises: Distinguish between what God commands us to do and what He promises to do. Both are important, but they serve different purposes in our lives.

Let Scripture Interpret Scripture

Use the Bible to interpret the Bible. When you encounter complex concepts or unclear passages, look for other places in Scripture where the same topics are addressed. Cross-references in your study Bible can help you find these parallel passages.

For example, when Jesus said in John 14:6, "I am the way, the truth, and the life: no man cometh unto the Father, but by me," He wasn't giving us one option among many. He was making an exclusive claim about salvation that's consistent with other biblical teachings about the uniqueness of Christ. Peter makes the same exclusive claim in Acts 4:12: "Neither is there salvation in any other: for there is none other name under heaven given among men, whereby we must be saved." Both passages teach the same truth: salvation comes only through Jesus Christ.

G is for Grow: Apply It to Your Life

Growth is where the rubber meets the road—where God's Word moves from your head to your heart and hands. This is where transformation happens, but proper growth always follows proper interpretation. As James warns us, "But be ye doers of the word, and not hearers only, deceiving your own selves" (James 1:22).

Ask the Right Questions

The wrong question to ask first is, "What does this mean to me?" The right question is, "What did this mean to the original audience?" Only after you understand the original meaning can you properly apply it to your life.

Once you understand what the passage meant to its original readers, ask these growth questions:

What does this teach me about God? Every passage of Scripture reveals something about God's character, His ways, or His will. What specifically does this passage show you about who God is?

What does this teach me about myself? Scripture has a way of holding up a mirror to our hearts. What does this passage reveal about human nature in general or your heart in particular?

Is there a sin to confess? Sometimes, the Holy Spirit uses Scripture to reveal areas of sin in our lives that need to be confessed and forsaken.

Is there a promise to claim? God makes many promises in Scripture, but make sure you understand who the promise was made to and under what conditions. Not every promise in the Bible is a universal promise for all believers.

Is there a command to obey? Look for clear commands that apply to all believers. Be careful not to turn descriptive passages into prescriptive commands, but when Scripture clearly commands something, take it seriously.

Is there an example to follow? Look for positive examples of faith, obedience, or godly character that you can emulate in your own life.

Is there a warning to heed? Scripture contains many warnings about the consequences of sin, unbelief, or disobedience. These warnings are given for our benefit and protection.

Make It Specific and Doable

Vague applications rarely lead to a life change. Instead of saying, "I need to love people more," try something specific like, "I need to speak more kindly to my spouse when I'm frustrated." Instead of "I should pray more," try "I will pray for ten minutes each morning before checking my phone."

The more specific your application, the more likely you are actually to follow through on it. Don't try to apply every possible lesson from a passage all at once. Pick one or two specific applications that you can actually work on. It's better to make small, consistent changes than to attempt major transformations that you can't sustain.

Consider Different Types of Growth

Application isn't always about changing your behavior. Sometimes, it's about:

Changing your thinking: Maybe the passage corrects a wrong idea you've had about God or challenges you to think differently about a situation.

Deepening your worship: Perhaps the passage reveals something about God's character that moves you to praise and thanksgiving.

Increasing your faith: Many passages are designed to strengthen our trust in God's promises and character.

Improving your relationships: Scripture has much to say about how we relate to God and others.

H is for Hear: Listen to the Holy Spirit's Voice

This is where you ask God to open your spiritual ears to what He wants to say specifically to you through His Word. As Jesus said, "He that hath an ear, let him hear what the Spirit saith unto the churches" (Revelation 2:7).

What Biblical Truth is the Spirit Revealing?

The Holy Spirit uses Scripture to reveal truths about God, ourselves, and others. As you study, ask:

"Holy Spirit, what are You showing me today about God's character?" "What are You revealing about my own heart and need for growth?" "How are You directing me to pray for or minister to others?"

This isn't about hearing audible voices or receiving new revelations outside of Scripture. The Holy Spirit speaks through God's Word, illuminating truths that are already there and applying them specifically to your heart and circumstances. Remember, this isn't about forcing God's Word to conform to your life and your current situation.

Different Ways the Spirit Speaks

Conviction: Sometimes, the Holy Spirit convicts you of sin, pride, or disobedience through the passage you're studying. Don't resist this conviction—it's evidence of His love and desire for your holiness.

Comfort: At other times, the Spirit brings comfort and encouragement through Scripture, reminding you of God's love, faithfulness, and promises during difficult seasons.

Correction: The Spirit may use Scripture to correct wrong thinking or redirect your path when you're heading in an unhelpful direction.

Calling: Sometimes, the Spirit uses Scripture to call you to specific action, service, or ministry opportunities.

Confirmation: The Spirit often uses Scripture to confirm decisions you're making or directions you're considering, providing peace and confidence in God's will.

Be Still and Listen

This step requires slowing down and creating space for spiritual sensitivity. After you've learned what the passage says, interpreted its meaning, and considered how to grow from it, take time to be quiet before God and ask what He wants to say to your heart specifically.

Don't rush this step. Sometimes, the Spirit's voice is a gentle whisper that requires patience and attentiveness to hear. Sometimes, He highlights particular aspects of the passage that are especially relevant to your current circumstances or spiritual needs.

T is for Trust: Respond with Faith and Obedience

The final step is Trust—responding to what you've learned with faith and commitment to obey. As Solomon wrote, "Trust in the Lord with all thine heart; and lean not unto thine own understanding" (Proverbs 3:5).

Write a Prayer or Confession of Faith

Close your study time by writing out a prayer that responds to what God has shown you. This might include:

Thanksgiving: Thank God for what He has revealed about Himself, His love, or His purposes.

Confession: Acknowledge areas where the Spirit has convicted you of sin or shown you a need for growth.

Commitment: Express your responsibility to obey what God has shown you and to trust Him with the outcomes.

Requests: Ask for God's help in applying what you've learned and for strength to live according to His truth.

Surrender: Submit your will to God's will as revealed in His Word.

Commit to Walk in Obedience

Trust means more than just agreeing with biblical truth—it means committing to act on it. Faith that doesn't lead to obedience isn't truly faith at all. As James reminds us, "Faith without works is dead" (James 2:26).

Make specific commitments about how you will trust and obey God based on what you've learned from the passage. These commitments should flow naturally from the growth applications you identified earlier.

Trust God with the Results

Sometimes, obedience to God's Word requires faith that goes beyond what we can see or understand. Trust that God will honor your obedience even when you can't see immediate results or when His commands don't make complete sense from a human perspective.

Remember that the goal isn't a perfect performance but a faithful response. God honors sincere efforts to obey His Word, even when our output is imperfect.

Putting It All Together: A Complete Example

Let me walk you through a complete LIGHT study using Philippians 4:6-7:

Learn: "Be careful for nothing; but in every thing by prayer and supplication with thanksgiving let your requests be made known unto God. And the peace of God, which passeth all understanding, shall keep your hearts and minds through Christ Jesus."

Key observations: "careful for nothing" (don't be anxious about anything), "every thing" (all concerns), "prayer and supplication with thanksgiving" (the method), "peace of God" (the promise), "shall keep" (God will guard).

Interpret:

- **Who**: Paul writing to the Philippians
- **What**: Instructions about handling worry through prayer, with a promise of God's peace
- **Context**: Part of Paul's teaching about joy and contentment in Christ
- **Meaning**: Instead of being anxious about anything, we should bring all our concerns to God through prayer and thanksgiving, trusting that His peace will guard our hearts and minds

Grow:

- **About God**: He cares about all my concerns, not just the "spiritual" ones. His peace is available to guard my heart and mind.
- **About me**: I tend to worry rather than pray. I often forget to include thanksgiving when I make requests.
- **Specific application**: When I start worrying about my job situation this week, I will stop and pray specifically about it, including thanking God for what He's already provided.
- **Command to obey**: Stop being anxious; pray about everything instead.

Hear: "Holy Spirit, I sense You're showing me that my tendency to worry reveals a lack of trust in Your care. You're calling me to bring my concerns to You immediately instead of carrying them as burdens. You want me to experience Your peace that surpasses understanding."

Trust: "Lord, I trust that You care about every concern in my life, even the small ones that seem insignificant. I commit to bringing my worries to You in prayer instead of carrying them alone. Help me remember to include thanksgiving in my prayers, not just requests. I trust Your promise that Your peace will guard my heart and mind when I bring my concerns to You. Give me the discipline to pray immediately when anxiety starts to rise. Amen."

Common Mistakes to Avoid

As you begin using the LIGHT method, here are some common pitfalls to watch out for:

Rushing Through Learning: Don't speed-read the passage to get to the "real" work of interpretation and application. The learning step itself is crucial—give it the time and attention it deserves.

Skipping Interpretation: Many people want to jump straight to the application, but this often leads to misapplication. Take time to really understand what the passage is saying before you try to apply it.

Making Everything About You: While application should be personal, remember that the Bible isn't primarily about you—it's about God and His plan of redemption. First, look for what the passage teaches about God, and then consider how it applies to your life.

Forcing the Spirit's Voice: Avoid manufacturing spiritual insights or forcing the "Hear" step. Sometimes, the Spirit's primary work is simply helping you understand and apply the clear meaning of the text.

Forgetting to Trust: Don't let your study end with good intentions. The "Trust" step requires a genuine commitment to obey what God has revealed to you.

Making Applications Too Vague: "I need to be more loving" isn't a helpful application. Be specific about what loving behavior you need to change or adopt.

Building the Habit

The LIGHT method only works if you actually use it consistently. Here are some practical tips for building this habit into your daily routine:

Start Small: Begin with just 15-20 minutes using this method. It's better to have a short, consistent study time than to burn out trying to do too much.

Keep a Journal: Write down your responses to each step of the LIGHT method. This helps you remember what you've learned and track your spiritual growth over time.

Find an Accountability Partner: Share what you're learning with a friend or family member who can encourage you and keep you accountable.

Be Patient with Yourself: You won't become an expert Bible student overnight. Give yourself time to get comfortable with the method, and don't get discouraged if some days seem more productive than others.

Adjust as Needed: While the basic LIGHT framework remains the same, feel free to spend more time on the areas where you need the most work. If interpretation is difficult for you, take extra time on that step.

When LIGHT Gets Easier

Like learning to drive, using the LIGHT method will eventually become second nature. You'll find yourself naturally asking learning questions as you read, looking for practical applications, listening for the Spirit's voice, and responding in trust and obedience. What once felt awkward and time-consuming will become a natural rhythm of encountering God through His Word.

But even when the method becomes familiar, don't let it become mechanical. The goal isn't to complete a formula—it's to meet with God through His Word. The LIGHT method is simply a tool to help you do that more effectively.

As you grow in your Bible study skills, you may want to add other methods and approaches to your toolkit. But LIGHT will always be a reliable foundation that you can return to whenever you need structure and focus in your study time.

Your Path to Biblical Illumination

The LIGHT method isn't just a study technique—it's a pathway to walking in God's truth every day. When you approach Scripture intending to learn carefully, interpret accurately, grow personally, hear spiritually, and trust obediently, you create space for God's Word to accomplish its intended purpose in your life.

Remember what God promised through the prophet Isaiah: "So shall my word be that goeth forth out of my mouth: it shall not return unto me void, but it shall accomplish that which I please, and it shall prosper in the thing whereto I sent it" (Isaiah 55:11).

God's Word has the power to accomplish His purposes in your life. The LIGHT method helps you position yourself to receive and respond to that powerful Word. As you begin using this approach, trust that the same God who inspired Scripture will help you understand and apply it to your life.

The psalmist declared, "Thy word is a lamp unto my feet, and a light unto my path" (Psalm 119:105). When you study Scripture using the LIGHT method, you're not just learning information—you're receiving divine illumination for your daily walk with God.

In our next chapter, we'll explore one of the most important principles for understanding any passage of Scripture: the crucial role of context. But for now, why not try the LIGHT method with a passage that has been meaningful to you? You might be surprised at what new insights God has waiting for you in familiar verses as you learn to walk in His light.

Study Questions for Chapter 4:

1. What aspects of Bible study have felt overwhelming to you in the past, and how might having a structured method like LIGHT help address those challenges?

2. Try the LIGHT method with Psalm 23. What did you learn that you might have missed in casual reading? How did listening for the Spirit's voice affect your understanding?

3. Why is it important to interpret what a passage meant to its original audience before applying it to your own life? Can you think of an example where someone might misapply Scripture by skipping this step?

4. How can the "Hear" step transform Bible study from an academic exercise into a personal encounter with God?

5. What practical steps will you take to build the LIGHT method into your

regular routine?

Practice Exercise: Choose one of these passages and work through the complete LIGHT method: Romans 8:28, James 1:2-4, or 1 Peter 5:6-7. Write down your responses to each step and share your insights with a friend or family member.

Chapter 5: Context is King

Have you ever walked into the middle of a conversation and completely misunderstood what was happening? Perhaps you've heard someone say, "I can't believe he did that!" and assumed they were angry, only to discover they were expressing admiration for someone's unexpected act of kindness. Without context—knowing who "he" was, what "that" referred to, and the speaker's relationship to the situation—you jumped to the wrong conclusion.

The same thing happens when we read the Bible without considering its context. We might read a verse that sounds encouraging and apply it to our lives, only to discover later that we completely missed what God was actually saying. Or we might read something that seems harsh or confusing because we don't understand the circumstances that prompted it.

Context truly is king when it comes to understanding Scripture. It's the difference between reading God's Word accurately and imposing our own ideas onto it. And here's the encouraging news: understanding context isn't as complicated as it seems. With a few simple principles and some practice, you can learn to read the Bible the way God intended it to be read.

What We Mean by Context

When we discuss context in Bible study, we refer to the circumstances that surround a passage, which help us understand its meaning more fully. Think of context as the frame around a painting—it doesn't change what's in the picture, but it helps you see it clearly and understand what the artist intended.

There are several types of context that affect how we understand Scripture, and we'll examine each one. But first, let me share why this matters so much.

Without proper context, we can interpret Scripture to mean almost anything we want it to mean. We can use it to justify our prejudices, support our political views, or excuse our sins. However, when we read Scripture in context, we allow God to speak for Himself rather than putting words in His mouth.

As Peter warned, there are those who "wrest" the Scriptures to their own destruction (2 Peter 3:16). The word "wrest" means to twist or distort. Context protects us from twisting God's Word and helps us understand what He actually said.

Immediate Context: The Surrounding Verses

The most important type of context is immediate context—the verses that come right before and after the passage you're studying. This is where most misinterpretation happens because people quote verses without considering what surrounds them.

Let me give you a classic example. You've probably heard people quote Jeremiah 29:11: "For I know the thoughts that I think toward you, saith the Lord, thoughts of peace, and not of evil, to give you an expected end." It's often quoted as a general promise that God has excellent plans for everyone's life.

But look at the immediate context. This promise was given specifically to the Jewish exiles in Babylon. God was telling them that after seventy years of captivity (verse 10), He would bring them back to their homeland. While the principle of God's goodness applies to all believers, this specific promise was given to a particular people at a specific time.

That doesn't make the verse less meaningful—it makes it more meaningful because we understand what God was actually promising and why.

How to Check Immediate Context

When you're studying a passage, always read at least the entire chapter, and preferably the chapter before and after as well. Ask yourself these questions:

What comes before? What topic was being discussed? What situation prompted this statement? What problem was being addressed?

What comes after? How does the writer continue the thought? What examples or explanations follow?

What's the flow of thought? How does your passage fit into the writer's argument or narrative?

Let's practice with a verse that's often taken out of context: "I can do all things through Christ which strengtheneth me" (Philippians 4:13). Taken alone, this sounds like a promise that Christians can accomplish anything they set their minds to.

But read the immediate context in verses 11-12: "Not that I speak in respect of want: for I have learned, in whatsoever state I am, therewith to be content. I know both how to be abased, and I know how to abound: every where and in all things I am instructed both to be full and to be hungry, both to abound and to suffer need."

Now, verse 13 makes more sense. Paul isn't saying he can accomplish any goal or overcome any obstacle through Christ's strength. What he is saying is that he can be content in any circumstance through Christ's strength. The context shows us that this verse is about contentment, not achievement.

Understanding this context doesn't diminish the verse's power—it focuses it correctly and helps us apply it appropriately to our lives.

Chapter Context: The Bigger Picture

Sometimes, you need to step back even further to understand a passage's meaning. Each chapter of the Bible was written for a purpose, and understanding that purpose helps illuminate individual verses.

Take Psalm 23, for example. Most people focus on the comforting images of green pastures and still waters, but the psalm is actually structured around the relationship between a shepherd and his sheep throughout their entire journey—from peaceful meadows to dangerous valleys to ultimate safety.

The chapter context reveals that this isn't just about God's provision during easy times but about His faithful care throughout all of life's seasons, including the difficult ones. Verse 4, "Yea, though I walk through the valley of the shadow of death, I will fear no evil: for thou art with me," isn't a separate thought—it's part of the continuous journey that starts with green pastures and ends with dwelling in the house of the Lord forever.

Finding the Chapter's Main Theme

When you start studying a new chapter, try to identify its main theme or purpose. Ask yourself:

What's the primary topic or issue being addressed?

What problem is being solved, or what question is being answered?

What's the main point the writer wants to communicate?

Sometimes, the chapter will have a clear topic sentence that tells you its purpose. Other times, you'll need to read through the entire chapter to discern the theme. Don't worry if it's not immediately apparent—practice makes this easier.

Book Context: Understanding the Author's Purpose

Every book of the Bible was written for a specific purpose and intended for a particular audience. Understanding this larger context prevents us from misapplying passages that were designed for particular situations.

For example, many of the commands in 1 Corinthians only make sense when you understand that Paul was addressing serious problems in the Corinthian church—divisions, immorality, lawsuits between believers, and confusion about spiritual gifts. His instructions weren't general principles for all churches in all times; they were specific solutions to specific problems.

This doesn't mean these passages have nothing to say to us today, but we need to understand their original purpose before we can properly apply their principles to our situations.

Questions for Understanding Book Context

Who wrote this book? Understanding the writer's background, personality, and other writings helps you understand his perspective and concerns.

Who was the original audience? Were they believers or unbelievers? Jews or Gentiles? What were their circumstances and challenges?

What was the writer's purpose? Was he correcting problems, encouraging faithfulness, explaining doctrine, or recording history?

When was it written? Understanding the historical timing can help explain why certain issues were important.

John tells us explicitly why he wrote his Gospel: "But these are written, that ye might believe that Jesus is the Christ, the Son of God; and that believing ye might have life through his name" (John 20:31). Knowing this purpose helps us understand why John selected certain miracles and teachings to include— they all support his goal of demonstrating Jesus' identity and mission.

Historical Context: When and Where It Happened

The Bible wasn't written in a historical vacuum. It was written by real people living in real places at real times, facing real challenges. Understanding these historical circumstances often explains why certain things were said or done.

For instance, when Jesus told His disciples, "And into whatsoever city ye enter, and they receive you not, go your ways out into the streets of the same, and say, Even the very dust of your city, which cleaveth on us, we do wipe off against you" (Luke 10:10-11), He was using a gesture that His Jewish audience would immediately understand. Shaking dust off one's feet was a symbolic way of saying, "We want nothing to do with you—not even your dirt."

Without understanding this historical context, the action might seem strange or meaningless. With it, we know that Jesus was giving His disciples a dramatic way to demonstrate the seriousness of rejecting God's message.

Key Historical Contexts to Consider

Political situation: Who was ruling? What was the relationship between Jews and Romans? How did political pressures affect daily life?

Religious climate: What were the Pharisees, Sadducees, and other religious groups teaching? How did their beliefs differ from Jesus' message?

Social customs: What were the accepted practices regarding marriage, business, worship, and social interaction?

Economic conditions: Were people prosperous or struggling? How did economic pressures affect their decisions?

Geographic factors: What was significant about the particular locations mentioned in the text?

You don't need to become an expert in ancient history, but paying attention to historical clues in the text itself will help you understand many passages more clearly. A good study Bible will often provide this historical background in its notes.

Cultural Context: Understanding Their World

Cultural differences between biblical times and our modern world can create significant barriers to understanding if we're not careful. What seems obvious to us might have been scandalous to them, and what was perfectly normal to them might seem strange to us.

Consider Jesus' encounter with the Samaritan woman at the well, as described in John 4. The text tells us that "his disciples marvelled that he talked with the woman" (John 4:27). Why were they surprised?

Understanding the cultural context reveals several barriers that Jesus crossed: Jews didn't associate with Samaritans, men didn't speak publicly with women they didn't know, and rabbis didn't engage in theological discussions with women. By speaking with this woman, Jesus deliberately broke cultural conventions to demonstrate the inclusiveness of His message.

Without this cultural context, we might read the story as a simple conversation. With it, we understand that Jesus was making a radical statement about the value and dignity of all people, regardless of their race, gender, or moral status.

Common Cultural Differences to Watch For

Family structures: Extended families were much more important in biblical times. When the Bible talks about "households," it often includes servants, extended family, and multiple generations.

Honor and shame: Biblical cultures were honor-and-shame cultures rather than guilt-and-innocence cultures like ours. Understanding this helps explain many interpersonal conflicts and social dynamics in Scripture.

Hospitality customs: Refusing hospitality was a serious insult. Understanding hospitality customs helps explain many biblical narratives.

Religious practices: Temple worship, sacrifice, ritual purity, and Sabbath observance were central to Jewish life in ways that are difficult for modern readers to appreciate.

Economic systems: Most people were farmers or tradesmen. There was no middle class as we understand it today.

Literary Context: Different Books, Different Styles

The Bible contains many different types of literature, and each type has its own characteristics and conventions. Reading poetry like you'd read a history book or interpreting prophecy like you'd interpret a letter will lead to confusion and misinterpretation.

When you read, "The trees of the field shall clap their hands" (Isaiah 55:12), you need to recognize that this is poetic language expressing joy, not a literal description of trees applauding. When you read Jesus' parables, it is essential to understand that they're stories designed to teach specific spiritual truths, not historical accounts of actual events.

Major Literary Types in Scripture

Narrative (Historical): Books like Genesis, Exodus, Joshua, 1 and 2 Samuel, and Acts. These tell stories, but often with theological purposes that extend beyond simply recording events.

Law: Leviticus, Numbers, Deuteronomy. These contain God's instructions for His people, though not all laws apply directly to Christians today.

Poetry: Psalms, Proverbs, Song of Solomon, and portions of other books. Hebrew poetry uses parallelism (saying the same thing in different ways) rather than rhyme.

Prophecy: Isaiah, Jeremiah, Ezekiel, Daniel, and the minor prophets. These often contain both immediate messages for the original audience and future predictions.

Wisdom Literature: Job, Ecclesiastes, Proverbs. These explore life's big questions and provide practical guidance for living wisely.

Epistles (Letters): Romans through Jude. These address specific churches or individuals with doctrinal teaching and practical instruction.

Apocalyptic: Revelation and portions of Daniel. These use symbolic language to describe ultimate spiritual realities and future events.

Each type requires slightly different reading strategies, which we'll explore more fully in our next chapter.

Biblical Context: Scripture Interprets Scripture

One of the most important principles of Bible interpretation is that Scripture interprets Scripture. The Bible is its own best commentary because it has one ultimate Author—God Himself. When you're trying to understand a difficult passage, often the best help comes from other biblical passages that address the same topic.

This principle is especially helpful when dealing with passages that seem to contradict each other. For example, Paul says, "For by grace are ye saved through faith; and that not of yourselves: it is the gift of God: Not of works, lest any man should boast" (Ephesians 2:8-9). But James says, "Ye see then how that by works a man is justified, and not by faith only" (James 2:24).

Do these passages contradict each other? Not when we understand their different contexts and let Scripture interpret Scripture. Paul is talking about how we're initially saved (by faith alone), while James is talking about how we demonstrate that our faith is genuine (by works that naturally follow).

Both are teaching aspects of the same truth from different angles.

How to Use Biblical Context

Look for cross-references: Most study Bibles include cross-references that point you to related passages. These can help you understand how different parts of Scripture relate to each other.

Study word usage: How does this writer use this particular word elsewhere? How do other biblical writers use it? A concordance can help you find other instances of important words.

Compare parallel passages: The Gospels often record the same events with different details. Comparing these accounts can provide a more comprehensive understanding of what happened.

Study theological themes: How does this passage relate to major biblical themes like salvation, sin, grace, or God's character?

Consider the concept of progressive revelation: God revealed His truth gradually throughout Scripture. Later revelations often clarify or expand on earlier revelations.

Practical Steps for Checking Context

Now that we understand why context matters and what types of context to consider let's discuss practical steps you can take to verify context in your Bible study.

Start Bigger, Then Go Smaller

Begin by understanding the larger context, then work your way down to the specific passage:

1. **Book level**: What's the purpose and theme of this entire book?
2. **Section level**: How does this chapter or group of chapters fit into the book's overall structure?
3. **Chapter level**: What's the main point of this particular chapter?
4. **Paragraph level**: How does this paragraph contribute to the chapter's theme?
5. **Verse level**: How does this specific verse fit into the paragraph's flow of thought?

Ask Context Questions

Develop the habit of asking these questions whenever you study a passage:

- What comes before and after this passage?
- What situation or problem prompted this statement?
- Who was the original audience, and what were their circumstances?
- What type of literature is this, and how should that affect my interpretation?
- Are there other passages that address the same topic?
- What would the original readers have understood this to mean?

Use Study Tools Wisely

While you can understand a lot of context just by careful reading, some study tools can help:

Study Bible notes often provide historical and cultural background that illuminates the text.

Bible dictionaries can explain customs, places, and concepts mentioned in Scripture.

Commentaries can help you understand how careful students of the Bible have interpreted difficult passages.

However, remember that tools should supplement your own careful reading, not replace it. Always read the passage carefully before consulting other sources.

Common Context Mistakes to Avoid

As you're learning to pay attention to context, watch out for these common mistakes:

Proof-texting: Using isolated verses to support a point without considering what they meant in their original context. This is probably the most common error in biblical interpretation.

Assuming universal application: Not every command in Scripture applies to all people at all times. Some were given to specific people in specific circumstances.

Ignoring the audience: Forgetting that biblical books were written to particular people with particular needs and circumstances.

Mixing contexts: Taking principles from one type of literature and applying them inappropriately to another type.

Modernizing too quickly: Jumping to modern applications before understanding what the passage meant to its original audience.

Over-spiritualizing: Finding hidden spiritual meanings in passages that were meant to be taken at face value.

When Context Changes Everything

Let me give you an example of how understanding context can completely change how we read a familiar passage. Many Christians quote Matthew 18:20: "For where two or three are gathered together in my name, there am I in the midst of them." This verse is often used to encourage small group meetings or to assure people that Jesus is present whenever believers gather.

But look at the context. The previous verses (15-19) are about church discipline—what to do when a fellow believer sins and refuses to repent. Jesus is giving instructions about confronting sin, bringing witnesses, and ultimately treating an unrepentant person "as an heathen man and a publican" (verse 17).

In this context, verse 20 isn't a general promise about small groups. It's a specific assurance that when church leaders gather to make difficult disciplinary decisions according to Jesus' instructions, He will be present to guide them. The "two or three" refers to the witnesses mentioned in the previous verses.

Understanding this context doesn't invalidate the general principle that Jesus is present when believers gather—that's taught elsewhere in Scripture. But it does help us understand what Jesus was specifically promising in this passage and avoid misapplying it.

The Reward of Careful Context

Learning to read Scripture in context requires more effort than just picking out encouraging verses, but the reward is worth it. When you understand context, you'll find that:

Difficult passages become clearer because you understand the circumstances that prompted them.

Apparent contradictions resolve because you see how different passages address different aspects of the same truth.

Applications become more accurate because you understand what God was actually saying before you try to apply it to your life.

Your confidence in Scripture increases because you see how consistent and reliable God's Word is when properly understood.

False teaching becomes easier to spot because you can recognize when someone is taking verses out of context.

Most importantly, you'll hear God's voice more clearly because you're listening to what He actually said rather than what you think He said.

Context and the Holy Spirit

Some people worry that emphasizing context makes Bible study too academic, leaving no room for the Holy Spirit's illumination. But the Holy Spirit doesn't bypass our minds—He works through them. He's the One who inspired the original writers to write in specific contexts for specific purposes, and He's the One who helps us understand those contexts today.

Jesus promised that the Spirit would "guide you into all truth" (John 16:13). Part of that guidance involves helping us understand the truth that God has already revealed in Scripture. The Spirit who inspired the Word is the same Spirit who illuminates the Word for us today.

Careful attention to context doesn't limit the Spirit's work—it creates space for it by removing the barriers that our assumptions and preconceptions can create.

Building Context Skills

Like any skill, reading Scripture in context gets easier with practice. Here are some practical ways to build this skill:

Start with clear passages where the context is obvious and straightforward. This will help you develop the habit of thinking contextually.

Practice with familiar verses that you've memorized. Go back and read them in their original context—you might be surprised at what you discover.

Study entire books rather than jumping around from verse to verse. This will help you understand how individual passages fit into larger arguments and narratives.

Ask context questions consistently until it becomes second nature.

Join a Bible study group where you can discuss your observations with others and share insights. Different people often notice different aspects of context.

The Foundation for Everything Else

Understanding context is foundational to everything else we'll discuss in this book. You can't properly apply Scripture until you understand its meaning, and you can't understand its meaning without considering its context.

In our next chapter, we'll explore how different types of biblical literature require different reading approaches. But all of those approaches are built on the foundation of reading in context.

As you continue your Bible study journey, remember that God wants you to understand His Word. He didn't inspire Scripture to confuse or mislead you, but to reveal Himself to you. When you take the time to understand context, you're showing respect for God's Word and positioning yourself to hear what He actually wants to say to you.

Context truly is king in Bible interpretation. When you understand the circumstances that surround a passage, you'll find that Scripture becomes clearer, more meaningful, and more applicable to your life. And that's exactly what God intended when He gave us His Word.

Study Questions for Chapter 5:

1. Think of a Bible verse you've heard quoted frequently. Now read it in its original context. Does understanding the context change how you understand the verse? How?

2. Why is it important to understand what a passage meant to its original audience before applying it to our modern situation? What problems might arise if we skip this step?

3. Choose one of the Psalms and identify as many types of context as you can: Who wrote it? What circumstances prompted it? What type of literature is it? How does this context affect your understanding?

4. How does understanding that Scripture interprets Scripture help us handle passages that seem difficult or contradictory?

5. What practical steps will you take to make checking context a regular part of your Bible study routine?

Practice Exercise: Take Matthew 7:1 ("Judge not, that ye be not judged") and study it using the context principles from this chapter. Read the entire chapter, identify the main theme, consider the audience, and see how this verse fits into Jesus' overall teaching. How does context affect your understanding of what Jesus meant by "judge not"?

Chapter 6: Different Books, Different Approaches

Imagine trying to read a cookbook the same way you'd read a love letter or trying to understand a poem the same way you would a newspaper article. You would end up confused and frustrated, missing the beauty and meaning that each type of writing was designed to convey.

The same principle applies to studying the Bible. While all Scripture is inspired by God and profitable for our spiritual growth, different types of biblical literature require different reading strategies. The approach that works beautifully for understanding one of Paul's letters might leave you scratching your head when you apply it to the book of Proverbs or the prophecies of Ezekiel.

Understanding these different literary types—what scholars call "genres"—will transform your Bible study from a one-size-fits-all approach into a toolkit of strategies that help you appreciate the unique beauty and message of each book. Don't worry; you don't need a seminary degree to master this. You already use these skills in everyday life when you automatically adjust how you read a text message versus a legal document versus a poem.

Why Literary Genre Matters

Before we explore specific types of biblical literature, let's understand why this matters for your Bible study. God chose to reveal Himself through a variety of literary forms because different types of truth are best communicated in different ways.

When God wanted to teach us about His faithfulness, He inspired David to write Psalm 23, using the beautiful imagery of a shepherd caring for his sheep. When He wanted to preserve the historical record of His dealings with Israel, He inspired the authors of 1 and 2 Kings to write detailed narratives. When He wanted to impart practical wisdom for daily living, He inspired Solomon to write the pithy sayings found in the book of Proverbs.

Each genre has its own distinct characteristics, its own method of conveying truth, and its own interpretive principles. Recognizing these differences will help you:

Ask the right questions for each passage based on what type of literature you're reading.

Avoid common misinterpretations that happen when people apply the wrong reading strategy to a particular genre.

Appreciate the beauty of how God has chosen to reveal different aspects of His truth.

Apply passages appropriately based on their intended purpose and style.

Historical Narrative: Learning from Stories

A large portion of the Bible consists of historical narrative—the books that tell the stories of God's people. This includes most of Genesis through 2 Kings, 1 and 2 Chronicles, Ezra, Nehemiah, Esther, and Acts, as well as portions of other books.

What Makes Narrative Special

Biblical narratives aren't just ancient history lessons. They're carefully selected and arranged stories that reveal God's character and His ways of working with people. As Paul reminds us, "Now all these things happened unto them for ensamples: and they are written for our admonition, upon whom the ends of the world are come" (1 Corinthians 10:11).

These stories teach us through example rather than through direct commands. They show us what faith looks like in real life, what happens when people obey or disobey God, and how God remains faithful even when His people are unfaithful.

How to Read Narrative Effectively

Focus on the main character's relationship with God. Biblical narratives are ultimately about God and His dealings with people. As you read, ask: What does this story teach me about God's character? How does God respond to faith, obedience, sin, or repentance?

Look for the moral of the story, but don't over-moralize. Biblical narratives often teach important lessons about life and faith. Still, not every detail of every story has a deeper spiritual meaning. Sometimes, a camel is just a camel.

Distinguish between description and prescription. Just because the Bible records that someone did something doesn't mean God approves of it or wants us to do the same thing. David committed adultery and murder, but these actions are recorded as examples of failure, not patterns to follow.

Pay attention to the narrator's point of view. The biblical writers often include subtle clues that help us evaluate the characters and events they describe. Look for phrases like "But David did that which was right in the eyes of the Lord" or "And the children of Israel did evil again in the sight of the Lord."

Consider the story's place in the larger narrative. How does this particular story fit into the overall account of God's relationship with His people? What role does it play in the larger storyline of Scripture?

Practical Example: The Story of Gideon

Let's apply these principles to the story of Gideon in Judges 6–8. As you read this narrative, notice:

God's character: Even though Israel has turned away from Him, God raises a deliverer when they cry out for help. He patiently works with Gideon despite his fears and doubts.

The main lesson: God can use weak, fearful people to accomplish His purposes. He often chooses to work through unlikely instruments so that His power, not human strength, receives the glory.

Descriptive vs. prescriptive elements: The fact that Gideon asked for signs doesn't mean we should put out fleeces every time we need to make a decision. This describes what Gideon did, not what we should do.

The larger context: This story fits into the cycle of sin, judgment, repentance, and deliverance that characterizes the book of Judges, showing both God's justice and His mercy.

Poetry and Wisdom Literature: Truth in Beautiful Language

About one-third of the Old Testament is written in Hebrew poetry, including the books of Psalms, Proverbs, Ecclesiastes, Song of Solomon, Job, and large portions of the prophetic books. This isn't poetry as we typically think of it—it doesn't rhyme in English—but it has its own distinctive characteristics that make it beautiful and memorable.

Understanding Hebrew Poetry

The key feature of Hebrew poetry is parallelism—the practice of saying the same thing in different ways or developing a thought across multiple lines. There are several types of parallelism:

Synonymous parallelism repeats the same idea in different words: "The Lord is my light and my salvation; whom shall I fear? The Lord is the strength of my life; of whom shall I be afraid?" (Psalm 27:1)

Antithetic parallelism contrasts opposite ideas: "For the Lord knoweth the way of the righteous: but the way of the ungodly shall perish" (Psalm 1:6)

Synthetic parallelism builds on an idea or completes a thought: "Trust in the Lord with all thine heart; and lean not unto thine own understanding. In all thy ways acknowledge him, and he shall direct thy paths" (Proverbs 3:5-6)

How to Read Poetry Effectively

Read for both the emotional tone and the content. Poetry engages both the mind and the heart. Notice whether the psalm is joyful, sorrowful, angry, or peaceful, and let that emotion inform your understanding.

Look for imagery and metaphors. Poetic language uses word pictures to help us understand spiritual truths. God is described as a rock, a fortress, a shepherd, and a father. Each metaphor reveals different aspects of His character.

Don't over-interpret every detail. When the psalmist says God will cover you with His feathers (Psalm 91:4), he's not teaching that God literally has feathers. He's using the image of a bird protecting its young to illustrate God's protective care.

Consider the structure. Many psalms have a clear structure that helps you follow the flow of thought—some move from complaint to confidence, others from praise to petition.

Practical Example: Psalm 1

Notice how this psalm uses contrasts (the righteous versus the wicked), metaphors (trees planted by rivers, chaff driven by wind), and a clear structure (describing the righteous man, then the wicked, then the outcome for each).

Wisdom Literature: Practical Truth for Daily Living

The wisdom books—primarily Proverbs, Ecclesiastes, and Job—approach truth from a different angle than historical narrative or prophecy. They deal with practical questions: How should we live? What principles lead to success and happiness? How do we understand suffering and injustice?

Understanding Proverbs

The book of Proverbs consists mainly of short, memorable sayings that express general principles about life. These are not absolute promises but practical observations about how life usually works.

For example, "Train up a child in the way he should go: and when he is old, he will not depart from it" (Proverbs 22:6) is a general principle about the importance of proper child-rearing, not a guarantee that every child raised in a Christian home will never rebel or struggle with faith.

How to Read Wisdom Literature

Look for general principles, not absolute promises. Wisdom literature teaches us about the normal patterns of life, but there are always exceptions to these patterns.

Consider the broader context of Scripture. The wisdom books focus on practical living, but they should be understood within the framework of the rest of the biblical revelation about salvation, grace, and God's sovereignty.

Apply the principles thoughtfully. Wisdom literature gives us guidelines for making good decisions, but we need to apply these principles wisely to our specific circumstances.

Practical Example: Ecclesiastes

This book takes an unusual approach, exploring life's meaning from a human perspective ("under the sun"). The Teacher's conclusion—that life without God is meaningless—drives us to find our ultimate satisfaction in the Creator rather than in created things.

Prophecy: God's Message Through His Messengers

The prophetic books can seem daunting to modern readers, but understanding their basic structure and purpose makes them much more accessible. The prophets were God's messengers, called to deliver His word to His people in specific historical circumstances.

Understanding Prophetic Literature

Prophetic books typically contain three types of material:

Messages about current situations: The prophets addressed specific problems in their own time—idolatry, injustice, unfaithfulness to God's covenant.

Warnings about future judgment: If people continued in sin, certain consequences would follow.

Promises of future hope: Beyond judgment lay restoration, blessing, and the ultimate fulfillment of God's promises.

How to Read Prophecy Effectively

Understand the historical context. Who was the prophet? When did he minister? What were the political and spiritual conditions of his time? This background helps you understand why certain messages were needed.

Look for the main themes. Most prophetic books emphasize God's holiness, the serious nature of sin, the certainty of judgment, and the hope of restoration for those who repent.

Distinguish between near and far fulfillment. Many prophecies had both immediate fulfillment (within the prophet's lifetime or soon after) and ultimate fulfillment (in Christ or the end times).

Pay attention to conditional vs. unconditional prophecies. Some prophecies were warnings that could be avoided through repentance (like Jonah's message to Nineveh), while others were unconditional declarations of what God would certainly do.

Practical Example: Isaiah 40

This chapter marks the beginning of the section in Isaiah that focuses on comfort and restoration. Notice how it moves from addressing immediate concerns (the Babylonian exile) to ultimate concerns (the coming of the Messiah). The "voice crying in the wilderness" found immediate fulfillment in John the Baptist but pointed toward Christ's first coming.

The Gospels: Four Portraits of One Savior

The four Gospels—Matthew, Mark, Luke, and John—are a unique genre that combines historical narrative with theological interpretation. They are not comprehensive biographies of Jesus but selective accounts designed to present different aspects of His identity and mission.

Understanding Gospel Literature
Each of the Gospel writers had a specific audience and purpose:

Matthew wrote primarily for Jewish readers, emphasizing Jesus as the promised Messiah and King.

Mark wrote for Roman readers, presenting Jesus as the suffering Servant who came to give His life as a ransom for the lost.

Luke wrote for Gentile readers, showing Jesus as the perfect Man and Savior of all people.

John wrote to demonstrate that Jesus is the Son of God, selecting specific signs and teachings to support this truth.

How to Read the Gospels Effectively
Consider each Gospel's unique perspective. When studying a particular event or teaching, consider why this Gospel writer included it and how it fits his overall purpose.

Look for the parallel accounts. Matthew, Mark, and Luke often record the same events but with different details and emphases. Comparing these accounts gives you a fuller picture.

Pay attention to Jesus' words and actions. The Gospels show us both what Jesus taught and how He lived, giving us a complete picture of His character and mission.

Notice the reactions of different people. How did the disciples respond? The religious leaders? The crowds? The responses often teach us important lessons about faith, pride, and spiritual understanding.

Practical Example: The Feeding of the Five Thousand

This miracle is recorded in all four Gospels, but each writer emphasizes different aspects of it. Matthew focuses on Jesus' compassion, Mark on the disciples' lack of understanding, Luke on Jesus' teaching ministry, and John on the significance of the signs in revealing Jesus' identity.

The Epistles: Letters with Lasting Relevance

The New Testament letters—from Romans through Jude—were written to address specific situations in early churches and individual Christians. Understanding their occasional nature (written for specific occasions) helps us apply their teachings appropriately to our modern circumstances.

Understanding Epistolary Literature

The epistles follow the standard format of ancient letters: greeting, thanksgiving or prayer, main body, and closing. But they're much more than personal correspondence—they're inspired Scripture designed to teach us how to live as Christians in the world.

Paul's letters typically follow a pattern: doctrinal teaching followed by practical application. Romans, for example, spends chapters 1-11 explaining the Gospel and chapters 12-16 showing how the Gospel should affect our daily lives.

The general epistles (Hebrews through Jude) address broader audiences and often focus on specific themes, such as perseverance through trials or warnings against false teaching.

How to Read the Epistles Effectively

Understand the original situation. What problems was the writer addressing? What questions had been asked? This background helps you understand why certain things were emphasized.

Distinguish between universal principles and specific applications. Some commands in the epistles apply to all Christians at all times, while others are specific to particular cultural situations.

Look for the theological foundation. The epistles typically root their practical instructions in theological truth. Understanding the "why" behind the commands helps you apply them appropriately.

Follow the argument. Epistles develop logical arguments and build from one point to another. Don't jump around randomly, but follow the writer's flow of thought.

Practical Example: 1 Corinthians

Paul wrote this letter to address specific problems within the Corinthian church, including divisions, immorality, lawsuits among believers, questions about marriage, and the use of spiritual gifts. Understanding these issues helps you see why Paul emphasized certain principles and how to apply those principles to modern church life.

Apocalyptic Literature: Symbolic Language for Ultimate Truth

The book of Revelation, along with portions of Daniel and a few other books, belongs to a distinct category known as apocalyptic literature. This genre uses very symbolic language to reveal spiritual truths about God's ultimate victory over evil.

Understanding Apocalyptic Literature

Apocalyptic writing typically includes:

Symbolic imagery: Numbers, colors, animals, and objects often have symbolic meaning rather than literal significance.

Visions and dreams: Truth is revealed through supernatural visions that require interpretation and careful consideration.

Cosmic scope: These books deal with ultimate questions about the end of history and God's final judgment.

Encouragement for persecuted believers: Apocalyptic literature was often written to encourage God's people during times of persecution by reminding them of God's ultimate victory.

How to Read Apocalyptic Literature

Don't over-interpret the symbols. While the imagery is meaningful, not every detail necessarily has deep symbolic significance.

Look for the main message. Despite its complex symbolism, apocalyptic literature usually has a clear central message: God will ultimately triumph over evil, and His people will share in that victory.

Consider the original audience. These books were written to encourage specific groups of believers facing persecution. Understanding their situation helps you grasp the book's primary message.

Let clearer passages interpret unclear ones. When dealing with difficult symbolic passages, let the clear teachings of Scripture guide your interpretation.

Practical Example: Revelation 1-3

The letters to the seven churches use symbolic language (candlesticks, stars) but also include clear, practical messages about faithfulness, compromise, and perseverance. This section shows how apocalyptic literature combines symbolic imagery with practical application.

Law: God's Instructions for His People

The books of Leviticus, Numbers, and Deuteronomy, along with portions of Exodus, contain the detailed laws that God gave to Israel. These laws served multiple purposes: they revealed God's character, set Israel apart from other nations, and pointed forward to the perfect righteousness that would be found in Christ.

Understanding Old Testament Law

The law included three types of regulations:

Moral law: Principles that reflect God's unchanging character (like the Ten Commandments).

Civil law: Regulations for governing the nation of Israel.

Ceremonial law: Rules about worship, sacrifice, and ritual purity.

How to Read Legal Literature

Look for the principles behind the specific commands. What do these laws reveal about God's character and His desire for His people?

Consider which laws apply to Christians today. The moral principles underlying the law are still relevant, but the specific civil and ceremonial laws were fulfilled in Christ.

See how the law points to Christ. The sacrificial system, the priesthood, and the emphasis on holiness all point forward to what Christ would accomplish for us.

Practical Example: Leviticus 19

This chapter includes both specific commands for Israel (like not mixing different types of cloth) and universal moral principles (like loving your neighbor as yourself). The key is discerning which commands reveal timeless principles and which were specific to Israel's unique situation.

Putting It All Together: A Genre-Sensitive Approach

Now that we've surveyed the major types of biblical literature, how do you put this knowledge to work in your Bible study? Here's a practical approach:

Step 1: Identify the Genre

Before you start studying a passage, take a moment to identify what type of literature you're reading. Is it a historical narrative, poetry, prophecy, or something else? This identification will guide your approach to the passage.

Step 2: Apply Genre-Appropriate Questions

Once you've identified the genre, ask the right questions for that type of literature:

- For narrative: What does this story teach about God and His ways?
- For poetry: What emotions and imagery are being used, and what do they reveal?
- For wisdom: What general principles for living are being taught?
- For prophecy: What was the historical situation, and what is God's message?
- For epistles: What specific situation is being addressed, and what universal principles apply?

Step 3: Consider the Genre's Characteristics

Remember that different genres communicate truth in different ways:

- Narrative teaches through example and story
- Poetry engages emotions and uses imagery
- Wisdom provides practical principles for daily living
- Prophecy calls for repentance and offers hope
- Epistles provide a theological foundation for practical living

Step 4: Apply Appropriately

Make sure your application matches the genre's intention:

- Don't turn narrative descriptions into prescriptive commands
- Don't literalize poetic imagery beyond its intended meaning
- Don't treat wisdom principles as absolute promises
- Don't miss the universal principles in culturally specific passages

Common Genre Mistakes to Avoid

As you develop your understanding of biblical genres, watch out for these common errors:

Flattening all genres into one approach. Reading the book of Proverbs like a legal document or the Psalms like a systematic theology textbook will lead to confusion and misapplication of its teachings.

Over-literalizing poetic language. When Jesus says He is the door (John 10:9), He's using metaphorical language to teach about spiritual access to God, not claiming to be made of wood and hinges.

Under-literalizing historical narrative. Just because some biblical language is symbolic doesn't mean all of it is. The Gospels record real events that happened in real history.

Ignoring cultural context in the epistles. Some commands in the New Testament letters were specific to particular cultural situations and need to be carefully applied to our modern context.

Making every detail of apocalyptic literature symbolic. While The Book of Revelation uses much symbolic language, some references (like the seven churches) refer to real places and situations.

The Beauty of God's Varied Revelation

One of the remarkable things about the Bible is how God has chosen to reveal Himself through such a wide variety of literary forms. He could have given us only a systematic theology textbook or only a legal code, but instead, He gave us stories that captivate our imagination, poems that stir our hearts, wisdom that guides our daily decisions, prophecies that warn and encourage, and letters that address our practical concerns.

This variety isn't accidental—it reflects the richness of God's character and His desire to communicate with every aspect of our humanity. When we learn to appreciate each genre's unique contribution, we gain a fuller, richer understanding of who God is and what He desires for our lives.

As the psalmist wrote, "O how love I thy law! it is my meditation all the day" (Psalm 119:97). When we understand how to read different types of biblical literature appropriately, we can join the psalmist in finding delight and wisdom in every part of God's Word.

Building Your Genre Recognition Skills

Like any skill, recognizing and appropriately reading different biblical genres gets easier with practice. Here are some practical steps for building these skills:

Study whole books rather than isolated passages. This helps you understand how different genres work and how they fit together.

Compare how different genres treat the same topics. For example, compare how the historical books, psalms, and prophets each talk about David's kingship.

Practice identifying genres in familiar passages. Go back to verses you know well and consider what type of literature they come from and how that affects their meaning.

Read carefully and thoughtfully. Don't rush through passages, but take time to notice their characteristics and consider how the genre affects your understanding.

Ask for help when you need it. A good study Bible or commentary can help you understand the background and characteristics of different biblical books.

Preparing for Deeper Study

Understanding different biblical genres is foundational to everything else you'll learn about Bible study. In our next chapter, we'll tackle one of the most common concerns beginning Bible students have: what to do when you encounter passages that seem confusing or difficult to understand.

But the principles you've learned in this chapter—recognizing different types of literature and applying appropriate reading strategies—will serve you well throughout your Bible study journey. They'll help you avoid common misinterpretations, appreciate the beauty of God's varied revelation, and apply Scripture appropriately to your life.

Remember, God didn't make His Word artificially complex. He used different types of literature because different types of truth are best communicated in different ways. When you learn to read each genre with understanding and appreciation, you're positioning yourself to receive the full richness of what God wants to teach you through His Word.

As Paul reminded Timothy, "All scripture is given by inspiration of God, and is profitable for doctrine, for reproof, for correction, for instruction in righteousness: That the man of God may be perfect, throughly furnished unto all good works" (2 Timothy 3:16-17). Every genre, every book, every passage has something profitable to teach us—when we know how to read it appropriately.

Study Questions for Chapter 6:

1. Think about a biblical passage that has confused you in the past. Now that you understand different genres, how might recognizing the type of literature help you understand it better?
2. Choose a psalm and identify the type of parallelism used (synonymous, antithetic, or synthetic). How does understanding this structure help you appreciate the psalm's message?
3. Why is it important to distinguish between description and prescription when reading biblical narratives? Can you think of an example where someone might misapply a narrative passage?
4. How does understanding that Proverbs contains general principles rather than absolute promises change how you read and apply these wisdom sayings?
5. What are the dangers of applying the same reading approach to all types of biblical literature? How can genre-sensitivity improve your Bible study?

Practice Exercise: Select one passage from each major genre (narrative, poetry, prophecy, epistle) and practice applying the appropriate reading strategies for each. Write down what you learn from each passage and how the genre affects your understanding and application.

III

Handling the Hard Stuff

Chapter 7: When You Don't Understand Something

Admitting that you are feeling confused by parts of the Bible doesn't make you stupid, unspiritual, or unqualified to study God's Word. It makes you honest. Even the apostle Peter admitted that some things in Paul's letters were "hard to be understood" (2 Peter 3:16). If an apostle who walked with Jesus found some Scripture difficult, you're in excellent company when you encounter challenging passages.

The key isn't to avoid difficult passages or pretend you understand everything. The key is to learn how to handle confusion constructively, distinguishing between genuinely unclear passages and those that seem hard simply because you're unfamiliar with them. Most importantly, you need to develop strategies that help you grow in understanding rather than giving up in frustration.

The Difference Between Hard and Unclear

Not all difficult passages are difficult for the same reasons. Understanding why a passage seems challenging will help you respond appropriately and avoid unnecessary discouragement.

Passages That Are Hard Because They're Unfamiliar

Many passages seem difficult simply because they contain concepts, customs, or historical references that are foreign to modern readers. These aren't actually unclear—they just require some background information to understand.

For example, when Paul writes, "Doth not even nature itself teach you, that, if a man have long hair, it is a shame unto him?" (1 Corinthians 11:14), modern readers might be confused because this doesn't seem true to us. But understanding the cultural context of first-century Corinth—where long hair on men was associated with certain pagan religious practices—clarifies Paul's meaning considerably.

These passages become clear once you understand their background. The solution isn't complicated; you need the correct information.

Passages That Are Hard Because They're Deep

Some passages are difficult because they deal with profound theological concepts that stretch our understanding. These passages aren't unclear—they're deep. The difference is important because it affects how you should respond to them.

Consider Paul's discussion of predestination and free will in Romans 9-11 or his explanation of how Christ can be both fully God and fully man in Colossians 1:15-20. These passages address mysteries that have challenged the greatest theological minds for centuries. They're not unclear because Paul was a poor communicator; they're challenging because they deal with truths that are at the limits of human understanding.

When you encounter these deep passages, don't expect to master them quickly. Instead, appreciate them gradually and return to them repeatedly as your understanding grows.

Passages That Are Genuinely Unclear

Some passages in Scripture are genuinely difficult to interpret with certainty. These might involve:

- Hebrew or Greek words that appear rarely and whose meaning is uncertain
- Historical references to events or customs that aren't fully explained

elsewhere
- Symbolic language in apocalyptic literature where the symbols aren't clearly defined
- Textual variants where ancient manuscripts differ slightly

For example, Paul's reference to people being "baptized for the dead" in 1 Corinthians 15:29 has puzzled commentators for centuries. We simply don't have enough information to be sure what specific practice Paul was referring to.

The crucial point is this: these genuinely unclear passages are relatively few and rarely involve essential doctrines. The main teachings of Scripture—regarding salvation, Christian living, God's character, and our eternal hope—are clearly taught in multiple passages. God hasn't left us to guess about the things we most need to know.

Strategies for Handling Difficult Passages

When you encounter a passage that is difficult to understand, here's a practical approach that will help you learn and grow rather than become discouraged.

Step 1: Don't Panic or Give Up

Your first reaction when encountering a difficult passage shouldn't be panic, embarrassment, or the assumption that you're not smart enough to understand the Bible. Remember that confusion is a natural part of the learning process. When you first learned to drive, you probably found it overwhelming to coordinate the steering wheel, pedals, mirrors, and traffic laws all at once. But you didn't conclude that driving was impossible—you practiced until it became natural.

The same principle applies to Bible study. Encountering difficult passages is part of the learning process, not evidence that you should quit.

Step 2: Slow Down and Read Carefully

Sometimes, passages seem more difficult than they actually are because we're reading too quickly or making assumptions about what they say. Before concluding that a passage is truly difficult, please take a moment to read it carefully several times.

Pay attention to:

- The exact words used
- The sentence structure and flow of thought
- Any connecting words (therefore, but, because) that show relationships between ideas
- The immediate context that surrounds the difficult verse or phrase

You might be surprised how often a careful, slow reading clarifies a passage that seemed confusing at first glance.

Step 3: Check Your Context

As we discussed in Chapter 5, context is important for understanding any passage. When you encounter something difficult, always check:

Immediate context: What comes right before and after this passage? How does it fit into the paragraph or section?

Chapter context: What's the main theme of this chapter, and how does this difficult passage contribute to that theme?

Book context: What was the author's purpose in writing this book, and how does this passage serve that purpose?

Many passages that seem confusing in isolation become clear when you understand their context. For example, Paul's statement, "I can do all things through Christ which strengtheneth me" (Philippians 4:13), seems to promise unlimited ability until you read it in the context of learning contentment in various circumstances.

Step 4: Use Cross-References to Find Parallel Passages

One of the most helpful strategies for understanding difficult passages is to find other Scripture passages that address the same topic. The Bible is its own best interpreter, and clearer passages often illuminate more difficult ones.

Most study Bibles include cross-references in the margins that point you to related passages. Use these to see how other biblical writers discuss the same themes, events, or concepts.

For example, if you're struggling to understand a particular parable in Matthew, check to see if Mark or Luke records the same parable with different details or explanations. If you're confused by a difficult verse in one of Paul's letters, look for other places where he discusses the same topic.

Step 5: Consider the Genre and Literary Style

Remember the principles from Chapter 6 about different types of biblical literature. Make sure you're reading the passage according to its proper genre:

- Is this poetry that uses metaphorical language?
- Is this historical narrative that describes rather than prescribes?
- Is this wisdom literature that gives general principles rather than absolute promises?
- Is this apocalyptic literature that uses symbolic imagery?

Many apparent difficulties disappear when you recognize that you've been applying the wrong reading strategy to a particular type of literature.

Step 6: Look for the Main Point

When you're struggling with details in a difficult passage, please step back and try to identify its main point. What is the central message the author is trying to communicate? Often, you can understand and apply the main teaching even if some details remain unclear.

For instance, the details of Ezekiel's vision in chapters 1 and 10 are complex and have been interpreted in various ways throughout the history of the church. But the main point is clear: God's glory and majesty are beyond human comprehension, yet He graciously reveals Himself to His people.

Don't let unclear details hinder your understanding of the main points.

When to Seek Additional Help

There's no shame in seeking help when you encounter passages that remain difficult despite your best efforts to understand them. In fact, God has given the church teachers and scholars to help explain His Word. The Ethiopian eunuch wasn't embarrassed to ask Philip for help understanding Isaiah—he was wise to seek assistance.

Study Bible Notes

A good study Bible can provide crucial background information that clarifies difficult passages.

Remember that study notes are helpful commentary, not inspired Scripture. They should supplement your own careful study, not replace it.

Bible Dictionaries and Commentaries

Bible dictionaries can provide explanations of people, places, customs, and concepts mentioned in Scripture. Commentaries provide verse-by-verse explanations of biblical books written by careful students of God's Word.

When choosing commentaries, look for authors who demonstrate reverence for Scripture and careful attention to the text. Some reliable options include Matthew Henry's Commentary, John Gill's Exposition, and commentaries by writers such as John MacArthur and Warren Wiersbe. Again, I have to emphasize that these are just fallible men who sometimes make mistakes. Their words and writings are not scripture.

Pastors and Mature Christians

Don't hesitate to ask your Pastor or other mature Christians for help with difficult passages. Most pastors are delighted to help church members who are seriously studying the Word of God. They can often provide insights from their training and experience that illuminate challenging texts.

Bible Study Groups

Sometimes, discussing difficult passages with other believers helps clarify your understanding. Different people notice different aspects of a passage, and group discussion can provide insights you might miss studying alone.

What to Do with Passages That Remain Unclear

Even after study and consultation with different resources, some passages may remain unclear to you. This is normal and shouldn't discourage you. Here's how to handle these situations constructively:

Focus on What Is Clear

When a passage contains unclear elements, focus on what you can understand clearly. Don't let the unclear parts prevent you from learning from the clear parts.

For example, Daniel's seventy-week prophecy in Daniel 9:24-27 has been interpreted in various ways by careful students throughout church history. But even if you can't settle all the interpretive questions, the clear message remains: God has a sovereign plan for history, He keeps His promises, and He will ultimately deal with sin and establish His kingdom.

Hold Your Interpretations Humbly

When dealing with genuinely difficult passages, hold your conclusions tentatively. Be willing to say, "This is how I understand this passage, but I recognize that other sincere students might interpret it differently." This humility is especially important for passages that don't involve core doctrines of the faith.

Continue Growing in Understanding

Many passages that seemed unclear to you as a beginning Bible student will become clearer as you grow in your knowledge of Scripture. The Bible has a way of interpreting itself as you become more familiar with its themes, patterns, and teachings.

Don't expect to understand everything immediately. Bible study is a lifelong journey of discovery, and God reveals His truth to us gradually as we're able to receive it.

Don't Build Doctrines on Unclear Passages

One of the most important principles of biblical interpretation is that unclear passages should be interpreted in light of clear ones, not the other way around. Don't build major doctrines or life decisions on passages that are genuinely uncertain in their meaning.

For example, the exact nature of spiritual gifts in 1 Corinthians 14 has been debated by sincere Christians; however, the clear teaching about love in chapter 13 provides the essential framework for understanding spiritual gifts, regardless of how one interprets the details.

Common Causes of Unnecessary Confusion

Many passages that seem difficult are actually made difficult by our own assumptions or approaches. Here are some common causes of unnecessary confusion and how to avoid them:

Reading Modern Ideas into Ancient Text

We sometimes make passages seem difficult by assuming they address modern concerns or use modern categories of thought. For example, when the Bible talks about the "heart," it usually refers to the center of thinking and decision-making, not just emotions as we might think today.

Try to understand biblical passages in their own historical and cultural context rather than imposing modern frameworks on them.

Expecting Scientific Precision from Non-Scientific Literature

The Bible wasn't written as a scientific textbook, and it uses observational language and phenomenological descriptions just like we do in everyday speech. When the Bible refers to the "four corners of the earth" or says the sun "rises," it's using ordinary human language, not making precise scientific statements.

Don't create unnecessary difficulties by expecting the Bible to conform to modern scientific terminology.

Over-Systematizing

Sometimes, we make passages difficult by trying to fit them into theological systems more precisely than the text itself warrants. While systematic theology is helpful, we shouldn't force biblical passages to answer questions they weren't intended to address.

For example, don't expect every passage about salvation to address every aspect of salvation. Let each passage make its own contribution without forcing it to be a complete systematic statement.

Perfectionist Expectations

Some Christians feel they must understand every verse perfectly before they can benefit from Bible study. This perfectionist approach leads to frustration and paralysis.

Remember that understanding Scripture is a gradual process. You can benefit greatly from passages even when you don't understand every detail perfectly.

Learning from Your Confusion

Interestingly, the passages that initially confuse you can become some of your most valuable learning experiences. Here's how to turn confusion into growth:

Keep a List of Questions

When you encounter difficult passages, write down your questions. This practice helps you remember what you want to study further and tracks your progress as you find answers over time.

Research Gradually

You don't need to solve every difficulty immediately. Make notes about passages you want to understand better and research them gradually as time and opportunity allow.

Celebrate Progress

When you finally understand a passage that once confused you, take time to appreciate your growth. This celebration motivates continued learning and reminds you that patient study pays off.

Help Others

As you learn to work through difficult passages, you'll be better equipped to help other believers who struggle with the same challenges. Your own experience with confusion makes you a more effective teacher.

The Role of Faith in Understanding

While careful study and good resources are important, don't forget that understanding Scripture ultimately depends on God's illumination through the Holy Spirit. Jesus promised His disciples, "But the Comforter, which is the Holy Ghost, whom the Father will send in my name, he shall teach you all things, and bring all things to your remembrance, whatsoever I have said unto you" (John 14:26).

This doesn't mean you should expect miraculous revelations to solve every interpretive difficulty. Instead, it means you should approach difficult passages with prayer, asking God to give you wisdom and understanding as you study carefully.

The psalmist prayed, "Open thou mine eyes, that I may behold wondrous things out of thy law" (Psalm 119:18). This should also be your prayer when facing challenging passages.

Maintaining Perspective on Difficult Passages

As you grow in your Bible study skills, it's important to maintain a proper perspective on difficult passages. Here are some crucial points to remember:

The Essential Things Are Clear

The important fundamental teachings of Christianity—the nature of God, the way of salvation, the principles of Christian living, and our eternal hope—are all clearly taught in multiple passages throughout Scripture. You don't need to understand every difficult verse to grasp what God wants you to know most.

Difficulty Doesn't Mean Error

The fact that some passages are difficult to understand doesn't suggest there are errors in Scripture. It simply reflects the limitations of our knowledge and understanding. As Isaiah reminds us, "For my thoughts are not your thoughts, neither are your ways my ways, saith the Lord. For as the heavens are higher than the earth, so are my ways higher than your ways, and my thoughts than your thoughts" (Isaiah 55:8-9).

Growth Takes Time

Understanding Scripture is a lifelong process. Don't expect to master difficult passages quickly or become frustrated when your understanding develops gradually. Even mature Christians continue to learn and grow in their understanding of God's Word.

Community Helps

God has given the church a community of believers who can help each other understand His Word. Take advantage of this community through Bible study groups, discussions with mature believers, and learning from pastors and teachers.

Building Confidence Despite Difficulties

One of the most important goals of this chapter is to help you build confidence in Bible study despite encountering difficult passages. Here's how to maintain confidence while acknowledging the challenges:

Start with Clear Passages

Build your confidence by spending significant time in passages that are clear and easy to understand. Books like 1 John, Philippians, and many of the Psalms provide rich spiritual nourishment without requiring extensive background knowledge.

Celebrate Small Victories

Notice when your understanding grows, even if it's incremental. When a passage becomes clearer through study, when you successfully apply a principle you've learned, or when you help someone else understand something—these are all victories worth celebrating.

Remember Your Purpose

Keep in mind that the goal of Bible study isn't to solve every interpretive puzzle but to know God better and grow in your relationship with Him. Many passages will accomplish this purpose even when some details remain unclear.

Trust God's Goodness

Believe that God wants you to understand His Word and that He will provide the understanding you need as you continue to study faithfully. He hasn't given you His Word to frustrate you but to guide and encourage you.

Practical Steps for Your Next Difficult Passage

The next time you encounter a passage that seems difficult or confusing, here's a practical checklist to work through:

1. **Pause and pray** for wisdom and understanding
2. **Read the passage slowly** several times
3. **Check the immediate context** (surrounding verses)
4. **Consider the broader context** (chapter and book)
5. **Identify the genre** and apply appropriate reading strategies

6. **Look for cross-references** to parallel passages
7. **Focus on the main point** rather than getting lost in details
8. **Consult study resources** if needed
9. **Ask for help** from mature believers if the passage remains unclear
10. **Apply what you can understand** clearly
11. **Be patient** with aspects that remain unclear
12. **Thank God** for what He has revealed through your study

Moving Forward with Confidence

Encountering difficult passages in Scripture is not a sign of failure—it's a normal part of the learning process. Even the greatest Bible scholars throughout history have wrestled with challenging texts and acknowledged areas where their understanding was limited.

What matters most is not that you understand everything perfectly but that you approach God's Word with humility, persistence, and faith. As you continue to study, you'll find that your understanding grows gradually and that passages that once seemed impossible become clear through patient study and spiritual growth.

The goal isn't to eliminate all difficulty from Bible study—that would make it less valuable for your spiritual growth. The goal is to develop the skills and confidence you need to work through difficulties constructively, learning and growing through the process.

Remember what God promised through the prophet Jeremiah: "And ye shall seek me, and find me, when ye shall search for me with all your heart" (Jeremiah 29:13). When you approach difficult passages with a sincere desire to understand and genuine commitment to obey what God reveals, He will honor that heart attitude and guide you into His truth.

In our next chapter, we'll look at another common source of confusion for Bible students: apparent contradictions in Scripture. We'll learn how to handle these challenging situations with wisdom and faith, building on the foundation we've established for dealing with difficult passages.

But for now, I encourage you to approach your next Bible study session with renewed confidence. When you encounter something you don't understand, remember that confusion is not failure—it's the beginning of learning. And the God who gave you His Word will help you understand what you need to know as you continue to seek Him with all your heart.

Study Questions for Chapter 7:

1. Think about a time when you felt confused or discouraged by a difficult Bible passage. How might the strategies in this chapter have helped you handle that situation differently?
2. What's the difference between passages that are "hard because they're unfamiliar" and passages that are "hard because they're deep"? How should you approach each type differently?
3. Why is it important to focus on what is clear in a passage rather than getting stuck on what remains unclear? Can you think of an example from your own Bible study experience?
4. How can maintaining a proper perspective on difficult passages help you grow in confidence as a Bible student?
5. What role should other believers (pastors, study groups, mature Christians) play in helping you understand difficult passages? How can you take advantage of this help without becoming overly dependent on others?

Practice Exercise: Choose a passage that has previously confused you and work through the ten-step checklist provided in this chapter. Write down what you learn at each step and how your understanding of the passage develops through this process. Don't worry if some aspects remain unclear—focus on what becomes clearer through careful study and analysis.

Chapter 8: Making Sense of Contradictions

One of the most challenging aspects of Bible study that every serious student will eventually face is apparent contradictions. These are passages that appear to contradict each other, creating confusion and sometimes doubt about the reliability of Scripture. They're the elephant in the room that many Christians are afraid to discuss openly. Yet, they're an inevitable part of honest Bible study.

Here's what I want you to understand from the outset: encountering apparent contradictions in Scripture doesn't mean you've discovered errors in God's Word. It usually means you've discovered opportunities to dig deeper into the text and grow in your understanding. Most apparent contradictions have reasonable explanations when sifted through with the right tools and perspective.

Why This Matters for Your Faith

Before we dive into specific strategies for handling apparent contradictions, let's address why this topic is so essential for your spiritual growth and confidence in Scripture.

It Strengthens Your Faith

When you learn to work through apparent contradictions carefully and find reasonable explanations, your confidence in Scripture actually increases rather than decreases. You discover that the Bible can withstand careful scrutiny and that apparent problems often lead to deeper insights into God's truth.

It Prepares You for Questions

Whether from skeptical friends, questioning family members, or your own honest study, you'll encounter challenges to Scripture's reliability. Learning to address these challenges thoughtfully prepares you to give a reason for the hope that lies within you.

It Teaches You to Study More Carefully

Working through challenging passages forces you to develop more effective study skills. You learn to pay closer attention to context, consider different perspectives, and think more precisely about what the text actually says versus what you assumed it said.

It Demonstrates Scripture's Depth

Many apparent contradictions disappear when you understand the richness and precision of biblical language. This process helps you appreciate the careful way God has preserved His truth in written form.

Common Types of Apparent Contradictions

Not all apparent contradictions are the same. Understanding the different types helps you approach each one with the right strategy and realistic expectations.

Different Perspectives on the Same Event

Many apparent contradictions arise when different biblical writers describe the same event from different perspectives or for different purposes. This is particularly common in the Gospels, where Matthew, Mark, Luke, and John each had distinct audiences and emphases.

For example, Matthew says the centurion came to Jesus personally to ask for his servant's healing (Matthew 8:5), while Luke says he sent Jewish elders to make the request (Luke 7:3). The apparent contradiction dissolves when you realize that in ancient culture, a person who sent representatives was considered to be acting personally through them. Both accounts are accurate from their respective perspectives.

Different Aspects of Complex Truths

Some apparent contradictions occur when different passages emphasize different aspects of the same complex truth. These passages aren't contradictory—they're complementary, like different angles of a photograph showing various aspects of the same scene.

Consider Paul's teaching about salvation. He writes, "For by grace are ye saved through faith; and that not of yourselves: it is the gift of God: Not of works, lest any man should boast" (Ephesians 2:8-9). But James writes, "Ye see then how that by works a man is justified, and not by faith only" (James 2:24). These passages seem contradictory until you realize they're addressing different aspects of salvation: Paul focuses on the root (how we're saved), while James focuses on the fruit (how saved people live).

Incomplete Information

Sometimes, apparent contradictions arise because we don't have complete information about the historical or cultural context. What seems contradictory to us might have been clear to the original audience, who understood the details we've lost over time.

Translation and Language Issues

Occasionally, apparent contradictions result from limitations in translation or differences between ancient and modern language use. Hebrew and Greek words sometimes have ranges of meanings that don't translate perfectly into English, creating apparent tensions that don't exist in the original languages.

Principles for Resolving Apparent Contradictions

When you encounter what seems like a contradiction in Scripture, here are proven principles that will help you work toward resolution:

Assume Scripture Is Consistent

Start with the assumption that Scripture is internally consistent, and that apparent contradictions have reasonable explanations. This isn't blind faith—it's a working hypothesis based on the Bible's track record of reliability. Countless apparent contradictions throughout history have been resolved through careful study, improved historical information, or a deeper understanding of the text.

This assumption doesn't mean you ignore difficulties or refuse to think critically. It means you approach apparent contradictions as puzzles to be solved rather than errors to be exposed.

Examine the Exact Wording

Many apparent contradictions disappear when you examine exactly what each passage says rather than what you thought it said. Read the passages carefully and precisely, paying attention to:

- The specific words used
- What is explicitly stated versus what might be implied
- Qualifications or conditions that might affect the meaning
- The scope of each statement (universal or particular)

For example, when Jesus says, "Ask, and it shall be given you" (Matthew 7:7), and John writes, "And if we ask any thing according to his will, he heareth us" (1 John 5:14), there is no contradiction. John's statement provides the crucial qualification that was implied in Jesus' teaching.

Consider the Context Carefully

As we've emphasized throughout this book, context is crucial for proper interpretation. Many apparent contradictions resolve when you understand the following:

- The immediate context of each passage
- The purpose of each book
- The audience being addressed
- The specific situation being discussed

The context often reveals that the passages address different situations, answer different questions, or serve different purposes.

Look for Complementary Rather Than Contradictory Perspectives

Train yourself to look for ways in which apparently contradictory passages complement each other. Often, what seems like disagreement is actually different writers providing different pieces of a larger puzzle.

Think of the blind men describing an elephant—one touches the trunk and says it's like a snake, another touches the leg and says it's like a tree, another touches the side and says it's like a wall. They're not contradicting each other; they're each accurately describing the part they can perceive.

Working Through Specific Examples

Let's apply these principles to some common apparent contradictions that trouble many Bible students.

Example 1: Has Anyone Seen God?

The apparent contradiction: John writes, "No man hath seen God at any time" (John 1:18), but Genesis says that Jacob "saw God face to face" (Genesis 32:30), and Exodus records that Moses and the elders "saw the God of Israel" (Exodus 24:10).

The resolution: These passages are talking about different types of "seeing." John is referring to seeing God in His full, unveiled glory—something that would be impossible for finite, sinful humans to survive.

The Old Testament passages describe theophanies (appearances of God in limited, veiled forms that humans could perceive without being destroyed). John himself clarifies this distinction when he adds, "the only begotten Son, which is in the bosom of the Father, he hath declared him" (John 1:18).

Example 2: Paul's Conversion Accounts

The apparent contradiction: In Acts 9:7, we read that the men traveling with Paul "heard a voice, but saw no man." But in Acts 22:9, Paul says they "saw indeed the light, and were afraid; but they heard not the voice of him that spake to me."

The resolution: The Greek language distinguishes between hearing a sound and understanding what is said. The men with Paul heard the sound of a voice but didn't understand the words Jesus spoke to Paul. Similarly, they saw a light but didn't see the person of Christ as Paul did. Both accounts are accurate when you understand these linguistic distinctions.

Example 3: Judas's Death

The apparent contradiction: Matthew says Judas "went and hanged himself" (Matthew 27:5), while Acts says he "falling headlong, he burst asunder in the midst, and all his bowels gushed out" (Acts 1:18).

The resolution: These accounts describe different aspects of the same event. The most likely explanation is that Judas hanged himself (as Matthew records), and later, the rope broke, or the branch gave way, causing his body to fall and burst open (as Luke records in Acts). Both writers describe accurate aspects of Judas's tragic end.

When Apparent Contradictions Remain Difficult

Even after careful study, some apparent contradictions may remain challenging to resolve completely. This is normal and shouldn't shake your confidence in Scripture. Here's how to handle these situations constructively:

Focus on the Clear Teachings

Don't let apparent contradictions overshadow the clear and consistent teachings of Scripture. The essential doctrines of Christianity—salvation by grace through faith, Christ's deity, the resurrection, and Christian living principles—are taught clearly and consistently throughout the Bible.

Remember the Limitations of Our Knowledge

We don't have complete information about ancient cultures, languages, and historical contexts. What seems contradictory to us might have been perfectly clear to the original audiences. Archaeological discoveries and improved understanding of ancient languages continue to resolve apparent contradictions that puzzled earlier generations.

Distinguish Between Core and Peripheral Issues

Not all apparent contradictions carry the same weight. Questions about exact numbers in census accounts or precise details of historical events don't affect core Christian doctrines. Keep these issues in proper perspective.

Maintain Intellectual Humility

Be willing to say, "I don't have a complete explanation for this apparent contradiction, but I'm confident that one exists." This isn't intellectual laziness—it's a humble recognition that finite minds don't grasp everything about infinite truth.

Common Mistakes to Avoid

As you work through apparent contradictions, watch out for these common errors that can lead to wrong conclusions:

Forcing Harmonizations

Don't invent elaborate explanations that stretch credibility to harmonize every detail. Sometimes, the simplest answer is that we don't have enough information to resolve an apparent contradiction completely.

Ignoring Context

Many apparent contradictions arise when verses are taken out of their proper context. Always consider what each passage is trying to accomplish within its larger framework.

Assuming Modern Precision Standards

Ancient writers didn't always aim for the kind of precise, technical accuracy we expect in modern academic writing. They often rounded numbers, summarized events, and focused on theological points rather than chronological precision.

Creating False Dilemmas

Don't assume that different emphases necessarily create contradictions. Two passages can emphasize different aspects of the same truth without contradicting each other.

The Role of Faith in Bible Study

Dealing with apparent contradictions requires a proper balance between faith and reason. This doesn't mean abandoning critical thinking, but it does mean approaching Scripture with trust in its ultimate reliability and authority.

Faith Provides the Framework

Faith gives you the confidence to study difficult passages carefully rather than abandoning Bible study when you encounter challenges. It provides a framework of trust that motivates thorough investigation rather than quick dismissal.

Reason Provides the Tools

God has given you a mind to use in studying His Word. Careful reasoning, attention to context, consideration of historical background, and logical thinking are all appropriate tools for Bible study.

The Spirit Provides the Illumination

Ultimately, understanding Scripture depends on the Holy Spirit's work in your heart and mind. Pray for wisdom as you study, trusting that God wants you to understand His Word and will guide you in that understanding.

Building Confidence Through Study

Working through apparent contradictions, rather than weakening your faith, can actually strengthen your confidence in Scripture's reliability. Here's how this process builds rather than destroys faith:

You Discover Scripture's Consistency

As you work through apparent contradictions and find reasonable explanations, you begin to see the remarkable consistency of Scripture despite its diverse authorship and composition over many centuries.

You Develop Better Study Skills

The careful attention to detail required for resolving apparent contradictions makes you a better Bible student overall. You learn to read more carefully, think more precisely, and study more thoroughly.

You Appreciate Scripture's Complexity

Working through difficult passages helps you appreciate the depth and richness of God's Word. You discover that the Bible can withstand the most careful scrutiny and actually rewards careful study with deeper insights.

You Become Better Equipped to Help Others

Your experience in working through difficult passages prepares you to help other believers who encounter similar challenges. You can share both the methods and the confidence that come from careful study.

Practical Steps for Your Next Apparent Contradiction

When you encounter what seems like a contradiction in your Bible study, here's a practical approach:

1. **Don't panic or immediately assume there's an error**
2. **Read both passages carefully** in their full context
3. **Note exactly what each passage says** (not what you think it says)
4. **Consider the purpose and audience** of each passage
5. **Look for possible complementary perspectives**
6. **Research the historical and cultural background** if needed
7. **Consult reliable study resources** for additional insights
8. **Consider whether translation issues** might be involved
9. **Focus on the main teaching** of each passage
10. **Be patient** if a complete resolution isn't immediately apparent

Resources for Further Study

When you encounter challenging apparent contradictions, several types of resources can provide helpful insights:

Study Bibles often include notes that address common apparent contradictions and provide background information that clarifies difficult passages.

Bible Dictionaries can explain historical, cultural, and linguistic information that illuminates challenging texts.

Apologetics Resources specifically address apparent contradictions and provide detailed explanations for common challenges to Scripture's reliability.

Commentaries by careful scholars often discuss interpretive challenges and provide various perspectives on difficult passages.

Remember that while these resources are helpful, they should supplement rather than replace your own careful study of the text.

The Bigger Picture

As you develop skills for handling apparent contradictions, keep the bigger picture in mind. The goal isn't to win arguments or prove intellectual superiority—it's to understand God's Word more clearly so you can know Him better and live more faithfully.

The vast majority of Scripture is clear and straightforward. The essential teachings about salvation, Christian living, God's character, and our eternal hope are taught consistently throughout the Bible. Don't let a few challenging passages overshadow the wealth of clear truth that God has provided for your spiritual growth.

Moreover, the process of working through difficult passages—including apparent contradictions—is part of how God grows us in wisdom, patience, and faith. These challenges aren't obstacles to overcome so much as opportunities to develop deeper trust in God and better skills for understanding His Word.

Moving Forward with Confidence

Apparent contradictions in Scripture are not threats to be feared but challenges to be embraced as part of your growing understanding of God's Word. When you approach them with the right principles and proper perspective, they become opportunities for deeper learning rather than sources of doubt.

Remember that countless sincere and careful students of Scripture throughout history have wrestled with these same challenges and emerged with a stronger, rather than weaker, faith. The Bible has proven its reliability through centuries of careful scrutiny, and it will continue to reward your careful study with increased understanding and confidence.

As you continue your Bible study journey, don't be surprised when you encounter passages that seem to contradict each other. Instead, be prepared to approach them as puzzles that can be solved through careful study guided by sound principles and empowered by the Spirit of God.

In our next chapter, we'll tackle another area that often confuses new Bible students: Old Testament laws and their relationship to modern Christian living. We'll learn how to understand which biblical commands apply to us today and which were specific to ancient Israel, building on the foundation we've established for careful, contextual Bible study.

The skills you're developing for handling difficult passages and apparent contradictions will serve you well throughout your Bible study journey. Most importantly, they'll help you approach God's Word with both confidence and humility, trusting in its ultimate reliability while remaining teachable and open to deeper understanding.

Study Questions for Chapter 8:

1. Why is it important to approach apparent contradictions with the assumption that Scripture is consistent rather than immediately concluding there are errors?
2. Think of an apparent contradiction you've encountered in your Bible reading. How might the principles in this chapter help you work toward a resolution?
3. What's the difference between "different perspectives on the same event" and genuine contradictions? Can you think of an example from everyday life that illustrates this distinction?
4. How can working through apparent contradictions actually strengthen rather than weaken your confidence in Scripture?
5. What role should faith play in Bible study when you encounter challenging passages? How do you balance faith with careful reasoning and study?

Practice Exercise: Research one of the apparent contradictions mentioned in this chapter (God being seen/not seen, Paul's conversion accounts, or Judas's death) using the ten-step approach provided. Write down what you discover at each step and how your understanding develops through careful study.

Chapter 9: Old Testament Laws - Do They Apply to Me?

Imagine a new believer who has just finished reading through the book of Leviticus for the first time. She comes to her Pastor with a notebook full of questions and a genuinely puzzled expression. "Pastor," she says, "I'm really confused. The Bible says I shouldn't eat pork or shellfish, that I need to make animal sacrifices for my sins, and that I can't wear clothes made of mixed fabrics. But I've never seen you sacrifice a lamb; I've seen you eat bacon, and I'm pretty sure your shirt is a cotton-polyester blend. Are we all disobeying God?"

Her honest confusion represents one of the most common struggles for Christians who seriously study the Old Testament. The first five books of the Bible contain hundreds of detailed laws covering everything from diet and clothing to worship and civil government. Some of these laws seem irrelevant to modern life (like instructions for treating leprosy). In contrast, others sound like they should still apply (like the Ten Commandments). But how do you tell the difference?

This question isn't just academic—it has practical implications for how you live your Christian life. Should you observe the Sabbath on Saturday or Sunday? Can you eat whatever you want, or are there still dietary restrictions in place? Do the financial laws about charging interest still apply? How you answer these questions affects everything from your weekly schedule to your dinner menu to your business practices.

Here's the good news: while this topic has complexities, it's not as confusing as it might seem at first. With a clear understanding of the different types of Old Testament law and how they relate to the New Covenant in Christ, you can navigate these questions with confidence and apply God's timeless principles to your modern life.

Understanding the Context of Old Testament Law

Before we delve into specific types of laws and their modern applications, it is essential to understand the broader context of why God gave these laws to Israel in the first place.

Israel as a Unique Nation

When God gave the law to Israel through Moses, He was establishing a unique nation that would serve several purposes in His plan of redemption. Israel was chosen to be:

A witness to the surrounding nations about the true God and His character. The law demonstrated God's holiness, justice, and mercy in practical ways that other nations could observe.

A repository for God's revelation through which He would preserve His truth and ultimately bring the Messiah into the world.

A picture of spiritual truths that would be fulfilled in Christ. Many of the ceremonial laws were designed to teach about sin, forgiveness, and God's holiness through concrete symbols and practices.

A practical society that could function as a theocracy under God's direct rule, with laws covering everything from worship to agriculture to civil justice.

Understanding these purposes helps us see why the law was so comprehensive and detailed. God wasn't just giving religious rules—He was establishing an entire society that would function as a light to the nations and a preparation for the coming Messiah.

The Temporary Nature of the Law

From the very beginning, the Old Testament law was intended to be temporary. Paul explains this clearly: "Wherefore the law was our schoolmaster to bring us unto Christ, that we might be justified by faith. But after that faith is come, we are no longer under a schoolmaster" (Galatians 3:24-25).

The law served as a "schoolmaster" (or tutor) to prepare God's people for Christ's coming. It taught them about sin, the need for forgiveness, the importance of holiness, and their inability to save themselves through perfect obedience. But once Christ came and fulfilled the law's requirements, the law's role as a tutor was complete.

This doesn't mean the law was bad or useless. Paul makes clear that "the law is holy, and the commandment holy, and just, and good" (Romans 7:12). The law perfectly reflected God's character and will. But it was never intended to be the permanent, final revelation of how God's people should relate to Him.

The Three Categories of Old Testament Law

To understand which Old Testament laws apply to Christians today, it's helpful to recognize that the law served three different functions, each with different implications for modern believers.

Moral Law: Reflecting God's Unchanging Character

The moral law consists of commands that reflect God's eternal, unchanging character. These laws aren't arbitrary rules but expressions of who God is—His holiness, justice, love, and truth. The Ten Commandments are the clearest example of moral law; however, moral principles also appear throughout the legal sections of the Old Testament.

Moral law includes principles like:

- Worshiping God alone and avoiding idolatry
- Honoring parents and legitimate authority
- Preserving human life and avoiding murder
- Maintaining sexual purity and marital faithfulness
- Respecting others' property and avoiding theft

- Speaking truthfully and avoiding false witness
- Being content rather than coveting what others have

These laws apply to Christians today because they reflect God's unchanging character. God's nature doesn't change, so the moral principles that flow from His nature remain constant across all ages and cultures.

However, the specific applications might look different in different cultures and contexts. For example, the principle of honoring parents is universal, but the particular ways children show honor to parents might vary between ancient Israel and modern America.

Ceremonial Law: Pointing Forward to Christ

The ceremonial law includes all the regulations about worship, sacrifice, priesthood, religious festivals, and ritual purity. These laws served several purposes:

They taught spiritual truths through physical symbols. The sacrificial system, for example, taught that sin requires death, that substitution is possible, and that God provides a way for sinners to approach Him.

They set Israel apart as God's chosen people. The dietary laws, clothing regulations, and purity codes made Israel visibly different from surrounding nations.

They pointed forward to Christ's coming work. Every sacrifice anticipated the ultimate sacrifice of Christ. Every priest served as a shadow of Christ's perfect priesthood. Every festival celebrated some aspect of God's redemptive plan that would be fulfilled in Christ.

The ceremonial law was fulfilled in Christ and no longer applies to Christians in its original form. As the writer of Hebrews explains, "For the law having a shadow of good things to come, and not the very image of the things, can never with those sacrifices which they offered year by year continually make the comers thereunto perfect" (Hebrews 10:1).

This doesn't mean we should ignore the ceremonial law. We can still learn from it about God's character, the seriousness of sin, and the wonderful work of Christ. But we don't need to observe these laws literally because Christ has fulfilled what they were designed to accomplish.

Civil Law: Governing Israel as a Nation

The civil law comprises regulations governing Israel as a political and social entity. These laws covered issues like:

- Property rights and inheritance
- Justice and punishment for crimes
- Economic relationships and business practices
- Treatment of foreigners and social outcasts
- Agricultural practices and land use
- Military service and warfare

These laws were specifically designed for Israel's unique situation as a theocracy in the ancient Near East. They don't apply directly to modern Christians because we don't live in the same political and social context.

However, the principles underlying these laws often do apply. For example, the specific regulations regarding the fair treatment of hired workers in ancient Israel don't apply directly to modern employment law; however, the principle of treating employees justly certainly does.

How Jesus Fulfilled the Law

Understanding how Jesus fulfilled the Old Testament law is crucial for knowing how it applies to Christians today. Jesus Himself said, "Think not that I am come to destroy the law, or the prophets: I am not come to destroy, but to fulfil" (Matthew 5:17).

Fulfillment Through Perfect Obedience

Jesus fulfilled the law by perfectly obeying all its requirements throughout His life. He never sinned, never broke any commandment, and perfectly reflected the righteousness that the law demanded. In doing so, He accomplished what no other person could achieve—complete obedience to God's standards.

This perfect obedience becomes the basis for our justification. When we trust in Christ, His perfect righteousness is credited to our account. We don't need to earn righteousness through law-keeping because Christ has already earned it for us.

Fulfillment Through Substitutionary Death

Jesus also fulfilled the law by bearing the penalty that our law-breaking deserved. The law demanded death for sin, and Christ died in our place, satisfying the law's just requirements. As Paul explains, "Christ hath redeemed us from the curse of the law, being made a curse for us: for it is written, Cursed is every one that hangeth on a tree" (Galatians 3:13).

Fulfillment Through Symbolic Completion

The ceremonial aspects of the law found their fulfillment in Christ's person and work. He became the ultimate sacrifice that all the animal sacrifices pointed toward. He serves as our great High Priest, making the Levitical priesthood unnecessary. His death tore the temple veil, symbolizing that we now have direct access to God through Him.

This is why Christians don't offer animal sacrifices or observe the ceremonial cleanliness laws. Not because these laws were wrong but because they accomplished their purpose of pointing us to Christ.

Practical Guidelines for Modern Christians

Given this understanding of the law's purpose and Christ's fulfillment of it, how should modern Christians approach Old Testament laws? Here are some practical guidelines:

Look for Underlying Principles

Even when specific Old Testament laws don't apply directly to modern Christians, they often contain principles that do apply. Ask yourself: What does this law reveal about God's character? What timeless principle is being expressed through this specific regulation?

For example, the Old Testament contains detailed laws regarding the treatment of servants and employees. While the specific regulations were designed for ancient Israel's economic system, the underlying principle—that employers should treat workers fairly and with dignity—certainly applies today.

Consider the Law's Category

Ask yourself whether a particular law is primarily moral, ceremonial, or civil. This categorization helps you understand how it might apply today:

- Moral laws generally apply directly, though the specific applications might vary
- Ceremonial laws have been fulfilled in Christ but still teach us about spiritual truths
- Civil laws were specific to Israel but often contain principles relevant to modern life

Pay Attention to New Testament Teaching

The New Testament provides crucial guidance about how Old Testament laws apply to Christians. When New Testament writers specifically address Old Testament laws, pay careful attention to their teaching.

For example, the New Testament clearly teaches that dietary restrictions have been lifted for Christians (Acts 10:9-16, 1 Timothy 4:3-5), that circumcision is not required (Acts 15, Galatians 5:2-6), and that we're not bound by ceremonial calendar observances (Colossians 2:16-17).

Focus on the Heart, Not Just the Letter

Jesus consistently emphasized that God is concerned with the heart behind our actions, not just external compliance with rules. In the Sermon on the Mount, He demonstrated how the moral principles underlying Old Testament laws extend beyond mere external obedience.

For example, the law said, "Thou shalt not kill," but Jesus taught that the principle goes deeper to include anger and hatred (Matthew 5:21-22). The law said, "Thou shalt not commit adultery," but Jesus taught that the principle includes lustful thoughts (Matthew 5:27-28).

This means that even when we understand the timeless principles behind Old Testament laws, we need to apply them with attention to heart attitudes, not just external behaviors.

Specific Examples and Applications

Let's work through some specific examples to see how these principles apply to common questions about Old Testament laws.

The Sabbath

The fourth commandment requires observing the Sabbath day and keeping it holy. This law is found in the moral law (the Ten Commandments) and also has ceremonial and civil aspects in its Old Testament applications.

The principle behind the Sabbath—setting aside regular time for rest and worship—reflects God's design for human flourishing and our need to depend on Him rather than constant work. This principle certainly applies to Christians today.

However, the New Testament makes clear that Christians aren't bound to observe the Sabbath on a specific day or in the exact manner prescribed by Old Testament law. Paul writes, "Let no man therefore judge you in meat, or in drink, or in respect of an holyday, or of the new moon, or of the sabbath days: Which are a shadow of things to come; but the body is of Christ" (Colossians 2:16-17).

Christians should apply the Sabbath principle by regularly setting aside time for rest and worship, but we have the freedom to choose which day and specific practices.

Dietary Laws

The Old Testament contains detailed laws regarding clean and unclean foods, forbidding the consumption of pork, shellfish, and many other foods that modern Christians often eat.

These laws served several purposes: they set Israel apart from other nations, they taught about holiness and separation, and they may have provided health benefits in the ancient world. But they were primarily ceremonial laws that pointed to spiritual truths about purity and separation.

The New Testament clearly teaches that these dietary restrictions no longer apply to Christians. Jesus declared all foods clean (Mark 7:19), Peter received a vision showing that God had cleansed previously unclean foods (Acts 10:9-16), and Paul taught that all foods are acceptable with thanksgiving (1 Timothy 4:3-5).

The principle behind these laws—that God's people should be holy and separate—still applies, but it's expressed through spiritual rather than dietary separation.

Financial Laws

The Old Testament contains numerous laws about economic relationships, including prohibitions against charging interest to fellow Israelites, require-ments for debt forgiveness every seven years, and regulations about fair business practices.

These laws were primarily civil laws designed for Israel's unique economic system, so they don't apply directly to modern banking and finance. However, they contain important principles about economic justice, care for the poor, and honest business practices.

Modern Christians should apply these principles by conducting business honestly, treating employees and customers fairly, and showing concern for those in economic need, even though the specific mechanisms might differ from Old Testament requirements.

Laws About Homosexuality

Old Testament laws clearly prohibit homosexual behavior, declaring it an "abomination" (Leviticus 18:22, 20:13). Some argue that these laws were purely ceremonial or cultural and don't apply to modern Christians.

However, these laws appear to be moral laws reflecting God's design

121

for human sexuality. This interpretation is confirmed by New Testament passages that also address homosexual behavior as contrary to God's will (Romans 1:26-27, 1 Corinthians 6:9-11, 1 Timothy 1:9-10).

The principle behind these laws—that God designed sexuality to be expressed within the bounds of marriage between one man and one woman—remains constant across both testaments.

Laws About Mixed Fabrics

Leviticus 19:19 prohibits wearing garments made of mixed fabrics (wool and linen together). This law seems arbitrary to modern readers and is clearly not observed by contemporary Christians.

This appears to be a ceremonial law designed to teach Israel about purity and separation. Like other ceremonial laws, it served its purpose of setting Israel apart and teaching spiritual truths, but it has been fulfilled in Christ and doesn't apply literally to modern Christians.

The broader principle—that God's people should avoid mixing what God wants to keep separate—might still apply in spiritual contexts, but not in the literal matter of clothing fabrics.

Common Mistakes in Applying Old Testament Law

As you work through questions about Old Testament law, watch out for these common errors:

All-or-Nothing Thinking

Some people assume that if any Old Testament laws still apply, then all of them must apply. Others assume that if some laws have been fulfilled in Christ, then none of them apply. Both extremes miss the nuanced way the New Testament handles Old Testament law.

The key is recognizing that different types of laws have different applications for modern Christians.

Cultural Relativism

Some interpreters dismiss any Old Testament law that seems culturally outdated, assuming that all laws were merely cultural rather than reflecting God's unchanging standards.

While cultural context is important for understanding how laws should be applied, don't automatically dismiss laws just because they seem foreign to modern culture. Some laws reflect God's unchanging moral standards that transcend cultural differences.

Legalistic Application

Others fall into the opposite error of trying to apply Old Testament laws in a legalistic manner without considering their purpose or Christ's fulfillment of them.

Remember that we're saved by grace through faith, not by law-keeping. Old Testament laws can guide our understanding of how to live faithfully, but they can't save us or make us more acceptable to God.

Ignoring New Testament Teaching

Perhaps the most serious error is ignoring what the New Testament says about Old Testament law. The apostles, inspired by the Holy Spirit, provide crucial guidance about how these laws apply to Christians.

Always consider New Testament teaching when determining how Old Testament laws should be understood and applied today.

The Heart Behind the Law

As you study Old Testament laws, remember that they all flow from God's character and His love for His people. Even laws that seem strange or harsh to modern readers were designed for Israel's good and to teach important spiritual truths.

The psalmist wrote, "O how love I thy law! it is my meditation all the day" (Psalm 119:97). He could love God's law because he understood that it reflected God's love for His people. The law wasn't a burden but a gift—a revelation of how to live in a way that pleases God and promotes human flourishing.

When Jesus summarized the entire law in two commandments—love God with all your heart, and love your neighbor as yourself (Matthew 22:37-39)—He was revealing the heart that beats behind every specific regulation. All the detailed laws were expressions of these two fundamental principles.

This means that even when specific Old Testament laws don't apply directly to modern Christians, they can still teach us about what it means to love God and love others. They show us God's concern for justice, holiness, compassion, honesty, and human dignity. They reveal His desire for His people to reflect His character in practical, everyday life.

Moving Forward with Wisdom

Understanding Old Testament law requires wisdom, careful study, and dependence on the Holy Spirit's guidance. Don't expect to resolve every question immediately or to have perfect clarity on every specific application.

Here are some practical steps for continued growth in this area:

Study Whole Passages, Not Just Individual Laws

Many Old Testament laws make more sense when you understand their context within larger passages. Read entire chapters or sections to know how individual laws fit into broader themes and contexts.

Learn from Church History

Throughout church history, faithful Christians have wrestled with these same questions. While church tradition isn't infallible, learning how previous generations understood these issues can provide helpful insights.

Focus on Clear Principles

When specific applications are unclear, focus on the clear principles that virtually all Christians agree on. Love God, love others, live honestly, show mercy, pursue justice, and maintain personal holiness.

Seek Wise Counsel

Don't hesitate to discuss challenging questions with pastors, mature Christians, or members of a Bible study group. Others may have insights that help clarify your understanding.

Apply What You Understand Clearly

Don't let uncertainty about some applications prevent you from obeying what is clear. There is plenty in God's Word that's crystal clear and ready for immediate application.

The Ultimate Goal

Remember, the ultimate goal in studying Old Testament law isn't to create a new legalistic system but to understand God's heart and character more clearly. The law reveals God's holiness, justice, mercy, and love. It shows us His concern for human flourishing and His design for healthy relationships and societies.

Most importantly, the law points us to Christ, who perfectly fulfilled its requirements and offers us the righteousness we could never earn through our own efforts. As Paul wrote, "For Christ is the end of the law for righteousness to every one that believeth" (Romans 10:4).

When you study Old Testament law with this perspective, it becomes not a burden but a blessing—a window into God's character and a reminder of how much we need the Savior who has fulfilled the law on our behalf.

In our next chapter, we'll move from understanding what Scripture teaches to applying it personally to our lives. We'll explore how to make the transition from Bible study to life change, ensuring that our growing knowledge of God's Word translates into growing conformity to God's will.

The foundation you're building in careful Bible study—understanding context, recognizing different genres, handling difficult passages, and correctly interpreting Old Testament law—prepares you for the crucial step of personal application. After all, the goal of Bible study isn't just to know more about God but to know God Himself and live in a way that pleases Him.

Study Questions for Chapter 9:

1. Why is it important to understand the different categories of Old Testament law (moral, ceremonial, civil) when determining their application to modern Christians?

2. How did Jesus "fulfill" the Old Testament law, and what does this mean for Christians today?

3. Choose one Old Testament law that initially seemed confusing to you. Using the principles from this chapter, how would you determine whether and how it applies to modern Christians?

4. What's the difference between the "letter" and the "spirit" of Old Testament law? How does this distinction affect how we apply these laws today?

5. How can studying Old Testament law actually help us understand God's character and grow in our relationship with Him?

Practice Exercise: Research the Old Testament laws about the Year of Jubilee (Leviticus 25:8-55). Identify whether these are primarily moral, ceremonial, or civil laws. What principles do they reveal about God's character and concern for justice? How might these principles apply to modern Christian living, even though we don't observe a literal Year of Jubilee?

IV

From Study to Life

Chapter 10: Making It Personal Without Making It All About You

I'll never forget the young man who approached me after a Bible study in our jail ministry, his eyes filled with genuine excitement. "Pastor," he said, "I just discovered something amazing in my quiet time this morning. When I read about how God provided water from the rock for the Israelites, the Holy Spirit showed me that this means God is going to provide the money I need for my legal defense. The rock represents my financial struggles, and the water represents the blessing that's coming!"

My heart sank a little as I listened to his enthusiastic interpretation. Here was a sincere believer who genuinely wanted to apply Scripture to his life, but he had fallen into one of the most common traps in Bible study: making everything about himself. He had taken a historical account of God's provision for Israel in the wilderness and twisted it into a personal prophecy about his legal needs.

This young man's mistake illustrates one of the most delicate challenges in Bible study: learning to apply Scripture personally without making it all about you. The Bible was written for us, but it wasn't written to us. It contains timeless principles that apply to our lives. Still, it isn't a collection of personal messages customized to our individual circumstances.

Finding the right balance between faithful interpretation and personal application is crucial for healthy spiritual growth. Apply Scripture too loosely, and you end up reading your own ideas into the text rather than learning what God actually said. Apply it too rigidly, and you miss the life-changing power of God's Word to transform your heart and circumstances.

The Foundation: What It Meant Then

Before any passage can be properly applied to your life today, you must first understand what it meant to its original audience. This is the non-negotiable foundation of all biblical applications. You cannot skip this step without falling into serious interpretive errors.

The Priority of Original Meaning

When Paul wrote to the Philippians, "I can do all things through Christ which strengtheneth me" (Philippians 4:13), he had a specific meaning in mind for a specific audience facing specific circumstances. Before applying this verse to your situation, you need to understand what Paul was telling the Philippians and the reasons behind it.

As we've seen in previous chapters, the context reveals that Paul was discussing contentment in various circumstances—being able to find satisfaction in Christ, whether he was well-fed or hungry, comfortable or suffering. He wasn't promising that Christians can accomplish any goal they set their minds to; he was testifying to the sufficiency of Christ's strength for any situation.

This original meaning doesn't make the verse less applicable to modern Christians—it makes it more applicable because it grounds the application in actual truth rather than wishful thinking.

Why Original Meaning Matters

Understanding original meaning protects you from several dangerous errors:

Eisegesis (reading into the text): Without understanding the original meaning, you're likely to read your own thoughts, needs, and desires into the passage rather than learning what God actually said.

False promises: You might claim promises that God never made or apply them in ways He never intended, leading to disappointment and weakened faith when expectations aren't met.

Cultural blindness: You may overlook important cultural and historical factors that influence how a passage should be understood and applied.

Doctrinal error: Building theology on misunderstood passages can lead to serious doctrinal mistakes that affect your understanding of God, salvation, and Christian living.

How to Determine Original Meaning

Use the tools and principles we've discussed in previous chapters:

Context: What was happening when this was written? What prompted these words? How does this passage fit into the larger argument or narrative?

Audience: Who was the original audience? What were their circumstances, challenges, and cultural background?

Genre: What type of literature is this? How should the genre affect your interpretation?

Cross-references: How do other Scripture passages illuminate this one?

Historical background: What historical, cultural, or linguistic factors help explain this passage?

Take the time to understand these factors before proceeding to the personal application. It's the difference between building on rock versus building on sand.

The Bridge: Timeless Principles

Once you understand what a passage meant to its original audience, you need to identify the timeless principles that bridge the gap between then and now. These principles reflect God's unchanging character and purposes and can be applied across cultures and centuries.

Identifying Universal Principles

Not every detail of every biblical passage contains a universal principle. Still, most passages contain at least one principle that transcends its original cultural context. Ask yourself:

What does this passage teach about God's character? God's nature doesn't change, so anything the passage reveals about His holiness, love, justice, mercy, or other attributes applies to all believers in all times.

What does this passage teach about human nature? Basic human needs, struggles, and tendencies remain constant across cultures and centuries.

What does this passage teach about spiritual life? Principles related to faith, obedience, prayer, spiritual growth, and the relationship with God are applicable universally.

What does this passage teach about relationships? Guidelines on how people should treat each other often contain universal principles, even when their specific applications may vary.

Examples of Universal Principles

Let's practice identifying universal principles in a few passages:

David and Goliath (1 Samuel 17): The original meaning refers to a specific historical event in which God delivered Israel through an unlikely champion. The universal principles include: God can use unlikely people to accomplish His purposes, faith in God overcomes seemingly impossible obstacles, and God receives glory when His people trust Him in difficult circumstances.

The Parable of the Talents (Matthew 25:14-30): Originally, Jesus was teaching about faithfulness in light of His coming kingdom. The universal principles include the following: God expects His people to be faithful with what He has entrusted to them, faithfulness in small things qualifies us for greater responsibilities, and accountability is a reality in spiritual life.

Paul's Instructions About Food Sacrificed to Idols (1 Corinthians 8): The specific issue of meat sacrificed to idols isn't relevant to most modern Christians, but the universal principles include: knowledge should be balanced with love, stronger Christians should consider how their actions affect weaker believers and love for others should sometimes limit our freedom.

Avoiding False Principles

Be careful not to create universal principles where none exist. Not every action by biblical characters is meant to be imitated, not every blessing promised to Israel applies to all believers, and not every specific command applies across all cultures and times.

For example, when God told Abraham to sacrifice Isaac, this was a specific test for a specific person at a specific time. The principle isn't that God might ask you to sacrifice your children but that God tests our faith and provides for our needs in unexpected ways.

The Application: Making It Personal

Once you've understood the original meaning and identified universal principles, you can begin applying the passage to your personal life. This is where the rubber meets the road—where God's Word begins to transform your thoughts, attitudes, and actions.

Ask the Right Questions

Instead of immediately asking, "What does this mean for me?" start with better questions that flow from proper interpretation:

How does this principle apply to my current circumstances? Consider your relationships, responsibilities, challenges, and opportunities. How might this principle guide your decisions or attitudes?

What changes does this principle require in my life? Be specific about thoughts that need changing, attitudes that require adjustment, or actions that need modification.

How can I practically implement this principle this week? Don't settle for vague resolutions. Identify concrete steps you can take to apply what you've learned.

What obstacles might prevent me from applying this principle? Anticipate challenges and plan how to overcome them.

How will I know if I'm successfully applying this principle? Identify measurable ways to evaluate your progress.

Types of Personal Application

Biblical application can take several forms:

Doctrinal Application: What does this passage teach me about God, salvation, spiritual life, or other important truths? How should this knowledge affect my beliefs and worldview?

Devotional Application: How does this passage encourage my faith, increase my love for God, or motivate me to worship? What does it reveal about God's character that should affect my relationship with Him?

Practical Application: What specific actions should I take as a result of this passage? How should it change my behavior, decisions, or priorities?

Relational Application: How should this passage affect my relationships with family, friends, fellow believers, or others? What changes do I need to make in how I treat people?

Ethical Application: What moral standards does this passage establish or confirm? How should it guide my ethical decisions in business, family life, or personal conduct?

Common Application Errors to Avoid

As you learn to apply Scripture personally, watch out for these common mistakes that can lead you astray:

The Fortune Cookie Approach

Some people treat the Bible like a fortune cookie, randomly opening it and expecting to find a specific message for their immediate situation. While God can certainly speak through any passage, this approach ignores the importance of context and proper interpretation.

Instead of seeking random messages, study passages systematically and look for principles that genuinely apply to your circumstances.

The Magic Formula Approach

Others treat biblical principles like magic formulas—if you follow these steps exactly, you're guaranteed specific results. This approach ignores the sovereignty of God and the complexity of life.

For example, Proverbs says, "Train up a child in the way he should go: and when he is old, he will not depart from it" (Proverbs 22:6). This is a general principle about the importance of proper child-rearing, not a guarantee that every child raised in a Christian home will automatically become a faithful believer.

The Direct Revelation Approach

Some Christians believe that every passage they read contains a direct, personal message from God for their specific situation. While the Holy Spirit does illuminate Scripture and apply it to our hearts, this approach can lead to reading meanings into the text that aren't actually there.

God speaks to us through Scripture, but He speaks through the actual meaning of the text, not through meanings we impose on it.

The Universal Autobiography Approach

This error assumes that every biblical character's experience should be duplicated in your life. If David was a shepherd who became a king, you should expect a similar dramatic rise in status. If Paul had a dramatic conversion experience, yours should be equally dramatic.

Remember that while Scripture contains patterns and principles, not every detail of every biblical character's life is meant to be replicated in yours.

The Cultural Blindness Approach

Some applications overlook the cultural and historical differences between biblical times and the present day. They apply ancient customs directly to modern life without considering how the underlying principles might be expressed differently in contemporary contexts.

For example, the biblical command to greet one another with a holy kiss (Romans 16:16) expresses the principle of warm, affectionate fellowship among believers. In our culture, this principle might be better expressed through heartfelt handshakes, hugs, or other appropriate demonstrations of Christian love.

Balancing Personal and Universal Application

The healthy biblical application requires balancing personal application with the recognition that Scripture's primary purpose isn't to address your individual concerns. Here are some guidelines for maintaining this balance:

Remember the Bible's Primary Purpose

Scripture's main purpose is to reveal God and His plan of salvation, not to provide personalized guidance for every life decision. As Paul wrote, "All scripture is given by inspiration of God, and is profitable for doctrine, for reproof, for correction, for instruction in righteousness: That the man of God may be perfect, throughly furnished unto all good works" (2 Timothy 3:16–17).

The Bible equips you for good works by teaching you about God, correcting wrong thinking, and providing wisdom for righteous living. Personal guidance is a beneficial byproduct, but it's not the primary purpose.

Focus on Character Before Circumstances

God is more concerned with developing your character than changing your circumstances. Look for applications that help you become more like Christ rather than applications that promise to make your life easier or more comfortable.

The goal of Bible study is spiritual maturity, not material prosperity or circumstantial comfort.

Consider Community, Not Just Individual Application

Many biblical passages are addressed to communities rather than individuals. Don't always make everything about your personal life. Consider how passages might apply to your family, church, or other communities you're part of.

Test Your Applications

Share your applications with mature Christians who can help you evaluate whether you're applying Scripture appropriately. Sometimes, what seems like a clear personal application to you might seem forced or inappropriate to others with more experience.

Be Specific but Humble

Make your applications specific enough to be meaningful, but hold them humbly. You might be wrong about how a passage applies to your situation, and you should be open to correction and refinement.

The Role of the Holy Spirit

The personal application of Scripture ultimately depends on the Holy Spirit's work in your heart and mind. Jesus promised that the Spirit would guide believers into truth and bring Jesus' teachings to remembrance (John 14:26, 16:13).

The Spirit Works Through Proper Interpretation

The Holy Spirit doesn't bypass the need for careful study and proper interpretation. Instead, He works through these processes to help you understand and apply God's Word correctly.

This means you should pray for the Spirit's guidance while also using your mind to study carefully and thoughtfully. The Spirit illuminates Scripture; He doesn't make careful study unnecessary.

The Spirit Convicts and Motivates

The Holy Spirit not only helps you understand how Scripture applies to your life but also convicts you of areas where change is needed and motivates you to make those changes.

When you read a passage and feel convicted about a particular attitude or behavior, that's often the Spirit working to apply God's Word to your heart.

The Spirit Provides Strength for Obedience

Understanding how to apply Scripture is only the first step. Actually making the necessary changes requires the Spirit's empowerment. As you depend on Him, He provides the strength to live according to God's Word.

Practical Steps for Balanced Application

Here's a practical process for applying Scripture personally while avoiding the errors we've discussed:

Step 1: Understand the Original Meaning. Use the interpretive tools from previous chapters to understand what the passage meant to its original audience.

Step 2: Identify Universal Principles. Ask what timeless truths the passage teaches about God, human nature, spiritual life, or relationships.

Step 3: Consider Multiple Applications. Don't settle for the first application that comes to mind. Consider doctrinal, devotional, practical, relational, and ethical applications.

Step 4: Make It Specific. Identify concrete ways to implement the principles in your daily life. Be specific about actions, attitudes, or decisions that you are taking.

Step 5: Plan for Implementation. Consider what obstacles you might face and how you'll overcome them. Create realistic plans for implementing your application.

Step 6: Seek Accountability. Share your applications with trusted friends or mentors who can encourage you and hold you accountable for following through.

Step 7: Evaluate and Adjust. After implementing your application, evaluate its effectiveness and make any necessary adjustments.

Examples of Balanced Application

Let's practice this process with a few passages:

Philippians 4:6-7: "Be careful for nothing; but in every thing by prayer and supplication with thanksgiving let your requests be made known unto God. And the peace of God, which passeth all understanding, shall keep your hearts and minds through Christ Jesus."

Original meaning: Paul encouraged the Philippians to manage anxiety through prayer rather than worry, promising that God's peace would guard their hearts and minds.

Universal principle: Christians should respond to anxiety and concern by bringing their needs to God in prayer, including thanksgiving for what He has already provided.

Personal application: "When I start worrying about my job situation this week, I will stop and specifically pray about it, including thanking God for the job I currently have and asking for His guidance about the future. I will look for God's peace to guard my heart instead of allowing anxiety to dominate my thoughts."

James 1:19: "Wherefore, my beloved brethren, let every man be swift to hear, slow to speak, slow to wrath:"

Original meaning: James was giving practical advice to early Christians about how to interact with others, particularly in the context of receiving God's Word.

Universal principle: Christians should prioritize listening over speaking and avoid responding in anger.

Personal application: "In my marriage, I will practice listening fully to my spouse before responding. When I feel my temper rising during discussions, I will take a moment to calm down before speaking. I will ask clarifying questions instead of making assumptions about what my spouse means."

The Ultimate Goal: Christlikeness

Remember that the ultimate goal of biblical application isn't to improve your circumstances or solve all your problems—it's to make you more like Christ. Every passage, properly understood and applied, should contribute to this overarching purpose.

As Paul wrote, "For whom he did foreknow, he also did predestinate to be conformed to the image of his Son, that he might be the firstborn among many brethren" (Romans 8:29). God's ultimate purpose for your life is to conform you to Christ's image. Scripture is one of the primary tools He uses to accomplish this purpose.

When you keep this goal in mind, it helps you maintain a proper perspective on biblical application. You're not looking for ways to manipulate God into giving you what you want; you're looking for ways to become the person He wants you to be.

Moving Forward with Wisdom

Learning to apply Scripture personally without making it all about you is a skill that develops over time. Don't expect to master it immediately, and don't be discouraged when you occasionally make mistakes in application.

The key is to approach Bible study with humility, recognizing that Scripture is God's Word, not your personal message center. Seek to understand what God actually said before determining how it applies to your life. Focus on becoming more like Christ rather than just improving your circumstances.

Most importantly, remember that application without proper interpretation is dangerous, but interpretation without application is useless. The goal isn't just to understand God's Word but to be transformed by it. As James warns, "But be ye doers of the word, and not hearers only, deceiving your own selves" (James 1:22).

In our next chapter, we'll focus on building sustainable Bible study habits that help you continue growing in your understanding and application of God's Word. We'll explore practical strategies for maintaining consistency in your study, overcoming common obstacles, and creating accountability systems that support your spiritual growth.

The foundation you're building in proper interpretation and balanced application will serve you well as you develop lifelong habits of engaging with Scripture. When you know how to study God's Word effectively and apply it appropriately, Bible study becomes not just an occasional activity but a transformative lifestyle that shapes every aspect of your Christian journey.

Study Questions for Chapter 10:

1. Why is it crucial to understand what a passage meant to its original audience before applying it to your life today? What problems arise when people skip this step?
2. What's the difference between a universal principle and a specific cultural application? How can you distinguish between them when studying Scripture?
3. Think of a Bible verse you've heard misapplied. How might understanding the original meaning and identifying universal principles lead to better application?
4. What role should the Holy Spirit play in biblical application? How do you balance dependence on the Spirit with careful study and interpretation?
5. How can focusing on Christlikeness as the ultimate goal help you avoid self-centered applications of Scripture?

Practice Exercise: Choose a familiar passage (such as Psalm 23, the Lord's Prayer, or the Golden Rule) and work through the seven-step application process outlined in this chapter. Write down what you discover at each step and how this systematic approach affects your understanding and application of the passage.

Chapter 11: Building Habits That Stick

One of the most honest conversations I've had about Bible study happened with a man in our church who had been struggling with consistency. "Pastor," he said with genuine frustration, "I've started Bible reading plans at least a dozen times. I'll go strong for a few days, maybe even a couple of weeks, but then something comes up at work, or I oversleep, or life gets crazy, and I miss a day. Then I feel guilty, try to catch up, get overwhelmed, and just quit altogether. I know I should be reading the Bible regularly, but I can't seem to make it stick."

Sound familiar? This man's struggle represents one of the more common challenges in Christian life: the difference between knowing we should study God's Word regularly and actually doing it on a regular basis. We recognize the importance of Bible study; we've personally experienced its benefits, and we genuinely desire to deepen our faith. But somehow, the demands of daily life, the pull of other activities, and our human weaknesses conspire to derail our best intentions.

The problem isn't a lack of desire or even a lack of knowledge about Bible study methods. The problem is that most people approach Bible study habits the same way they approach New Year's resolutions—with enthusiasm but without a realistic plan for long-term success. They set ambitious goals, depend on willpower alone, and abandon their efforts at the first sign of difficulty.

But building lasting Bible study habits doesn't have to be this frustrating. With the right approach, realistic expectations, and practical strategies, you can cultivate a sustainable pattern of engagement with God's Word that withstands the inevitable challenges of real life. The key is understanding how habits actually form and applying proven principles that work with human nature rather than against it.

Understanding How Habits Work

Before we look into specific strategies for Bible study habits, it will be helpful to understand the basic mechanics of how a habit forms. This knowledge will help you work with your brain's natural patterns rather than fighting against them.

The Habit Loop

Researchers have discovered that all habits follow a three-part pattern called the habit loop:

Cue: A trigger that tells your brain to go into automatic mode and which habit to use. This might be a specific time of day, a particular location, an intense emotion, or another activity.

Routine: The behavior itself—the physical, mental, or emotional pattern that follows the cue.

Reward: The benefit you gain from completing the routine, which helps your brain remember the habit loop for the future.

Understanding this loop is crucial for building Bible study habits because it helps you identify what triggers your study time, what the actual study routine involves, and what rewards motivate you to continue.

The Role of Consistency

Habits become automatic through repetition, not intensity. Studying the Bible for three hours once a week is less effective for forming a habit than studying for fifteen minutes every day. Your brain learns patterns through consistent repetition, so regular, smaller efforts will build stronger habits than sporadic, heroic efforts.

This is why the "all-or-nothing" approach so often fails. When people miss their ambitious study goals, they feel like failures and abandon their efforts entirely. But if your goal is small and manageable, missing one day doesn't derail the entire enterprise.

The Power of Environment

Your physical environment plays a major role in habit formation. If you always study in the same place at the same time with the same setup, these environmental cues will eventually trigger the study behavior automatically. Conversely, if you're constantly changing when, where, and how you study, your brain never develops the automatic patterns that make habits stick.

Starting Small and Building Momentum

The biggest mistake most people make when trying to establish Bible study habits is starting too big. They decide they're going to read five chapters a day, study for an hour every morning, and work through the entire Bible in six months. These ambitious goals almost always lead to failure and discouragement.

The Power of Starting Small

Instead of trying to become a Bible study expert overnight, start with something so small it feels almost laughably easy. Here are some examples of good starting points:

- Read one psalm every day
- Study one verse using the LIGHT method
- Read for five minutes before breakfast
- Listen to one chapter of the Bible during your commute
- Read three verses and write down one observation

The goal isn't to accomplish a lot initially—it's to establish the pattern. Once you've successfully maintained a small habit for several weeks, you can gradually increase the difficulty or duration.

Why Small Starts Work

Starting small works for several psychological reasons:

It reduces resistance: When a task feels manageable, you're less likely to procrastinate or make excuses.

It builds confidence: Early successes create momentum and confidence that motivate you to continue.

It establishes the neural pathways: Even small amounts of repetition begin to create the automatic patterns that characterize habits.

It allows for growth: It's easier to expand an existing habit than to create a new one from scratch.

Building on Success

Once you've successfully maintained a small Bible study habit for about three weeks, you can begin to expand it gradually. Add five minutes to your study time, include an additional element to your routine, or tackle slightly longer passages. The key is to expand slowly enough that the new level feels manageable.

For example, if you've been successfully reading one psalm daily for three weeks, you might add one proverb to create a psalm-and-proverb routine. After another few weeks, consider including a few observations about what you've read. Each expansion should feel like a natural next step, not a dramatic increase in difficulty.

Overcoming Common Obstacles

Even with the best intentions and realistic goals, you'll face obstacles that threaten to derail your Bible study habits. Anticipating these challenges and having strategies ready to address them will help you persevere through difficult periods.

The Time Challenge

"I don't have time" is the most common excuse for inconsistent Bible study, and it's often valid. Life is busy, schedules are packed, and unexpected demands constantly arise. Let's look at some strategies for overcoming time constraints:

Find existing pockets of time: Instead of trying to create new time, look for existing time you could use more productively. Most people have small pockets of time throughout the day that could accommodate brief Bible study—waiting in line, commuting, eating breakfast alone, or the few minutes before falling asleep.

Replace less valuable activities: Honestly evaluate how you spend your time and identify activities you could reduce or eliminate. Could you study the Bible instead of scrolling social media for ten minutes? Could you listen to Scripture during your workout instead of music?

Link to existing routines: Attach Bible study to something you already do consistently. Read a few verses while drinking your morning coffee, study during lunch, or read a psalm before brushing your teeth at night.

Use technology wisely: Bible apps allow you to study during previously unusable times—waiting for appointments, standing in line, or during short breaks at work.

The Motivation Challenge

Initial enthusiasm for Bible study often wanes when the routine becomes, well, routine. Here's how to maintain motivation over the long term:

Remember your why: Regularly remind yourself why Bible study matters. Keep a list of benefits you've experienced, verses that have encouraged you, or insights that have helped you grow.

Celebrate small wins: Acknowledge when you successfully maintain your habit, even for short periods. Completed weeks, meaningful insights, or moments when Scripture helped you through difficulty are all worth celebrating.

Track your progress: Keep a record of your study. This might be as simple as marking a calendar or keeping a basic journal. Seeing a visual record of your progress provides motivation to continue.

Vary your approach: Prevent boredom by occasionally changing your study method, Bible translation, or focus. You might alternate between narrative books and epistles or between devotional reading and more analytical study.

The Guilt Challenge

Many people abandon Bible study habits because they feel guilty when they miss days or don't understand what they're reading. This guilt often becomes a bigger obstacle than the original problem.

Expect imperfection: Accept from the beginning that you won't be perfect. You'll miss days, you'll struggle with difficult passages, and you'll sometimes feel like you're not getting much out of your study. This is normal, not failure.

Focus on progress, not perfection: Instead of aiming for a perfect record, aim for overall improvement. If you studied the Bible ten days this month compared to three days last month, that's significant progress worth celebrating.

Get back on track quickly: When you miss a day (or several days), don't try to catch up by doing extra reading. Simply resume your regular routine. The goal is consistency, not completion of a predetermined amount of material.

Learn from setbacks: When your habit gets derailed, take time to understand why. Was your goal too ambitious? Did your schedule change? Did you lose motivation? Use this information to adjust your approach rather than just trying harder with the same methods.

Creating Your Ideal Study Environment

Your environment significantly impacts your ability to concentrate and maintain consistent study habits. While you don't need a perfect setup to study effectively, thoughtful attention to your environment can make a substantial difference.

Choose Your Location Wisely

Select a specific place for Bible study and use it consistently. This location becomes an environmental cue that triggers your study routine automatically. Consider these factors when choosing your spot:

Minimal distractions: Avoid places where you're likely to be interrupted or tempted by other activities. If you study at the kitchen table, you might be distracted by dishes that need washing or preparations for the day.

Comfortable but not too comfortable: You want to be physically comfortable enough to concentrate but not so comfortable that you're tempted to fall asleep or lose focus.

Good lighting: Adequate lighting is easier on the eyes and helps maintain alertness, especially during early morning or evening study times.

Associated with focus: If possible, choose a location you associate with concentration and thoughtful activity rather than relaxation or entertainment.

Organize Your Materials

Keep your Bible study materials organized and easily accessible. Having to search for your Bible, notebook, or pen creates friction that makes it easier to skip your study time. Consider creating a simple "study kit" that includes:

- Your primary Bible
- A notebook or journal for observations and applications
- A pen or pencil
- Any study tools you use regularly (concordance, study Bible, etc.)

Minimize Digital Distractions

If you use digital tools for Bible study, be intentional about minimizing distractions. Turn off notifications, close unnecessary apps, and resist the urge to check your email or social media during study time. Many people find that starting with physical books helps establish the habit before introducing digital tools.

Make It Inviting

Your study space should feel welcoming and peaceful. This might mean adding a plant, increasing ventilation, or including some Christian artwork. The goal is to create an environment that draws you in rather than one you want to escape.

Accountability and Community Support

While Bible study is often a personal activity, having support from others significantly increases your chances of maintaining consistent habits. Humans are social creatures, and we're more likely to follow through on commitments when others are involved.

Types of Accountability

Study partner: Find someone who's also working to develop Bible study habits and check in with each other regularly. You might study the same passages and discuss your insights or simply encourage each other to maintain consistency.

Small group: Join or form a Bible study group that provides natural accountability. When you know others are expecting you to have read certain passages or worked through specific questions, you're more motivated to follow through.

Mentor or mature Christian: Ask a spiritually mature person to check in with you about your Bible study habits. They can provide encouragement, answer questions, and help you work through challenges.

Family accountability: If you're married or have children old enough to participate, create family Bible study times or share what you're learning with family members.

Making Accountability Work

Be specific about expectations: Clearly define what you're asking for from your accountability partners. Do you want them to ask about your consistency? Your insights? Your applications?

Regular check-ins: Create a regular schedule for accountability conversations—weekly coffee, monthly phone calls, or brief text exchanges.

Honest communication: Be truthful about your struggles and successes. Accountability only works when it's based on honest self-assessment and open communication.

Mutual encouragement: The best accountability relationships involve mutual support rather than one-way reporting. Everyone benefits from encouragement and shared wisdom.

Dealing with Seasons of Difficulty

Even with good habits and strong accountability, you'll encounter seasons when Bible study feels particularly difficult. Recognizing these challenging periods and having strategies to navigate them helps prevent temporary struggles from becoming permanent abandonment of your habits.

Common Difficult Seasons

Life transitions: Starting a new job, moving to a new home, getting married, having children, or other major life changes can disrupt established routines.

Spiritual dryness: Periods when Bible study feels mechanical or unrewarding are normal parts of the Christian journey but can threaten motivation.

Increased busyness: Work deadlines, family crises, health challenges, or other demands can squeeze out time for Bible study.

Intellectual struggles: Encountering difficult passages, apparent contradictions, or challenging doctrines can create doubt and confusion that affect motivation.

Strategies for Difficult Seasons

Reduce but don't eliminate: During challenging periods, scale back your Bible study routine rather than abandoning it entirely. Even five minutes of reading or one verse of reflection maintains the habit and keeps you connected to God's Word.

Focus on encouragement: During difficult seasons, prioritize passages that comfort, encourage, and strengthen rather than those that challenge or convict. Psalms, the Gospels, and encouraging epistles like Philippians can provide the spiritual nourishment you need.

Seek extra support: Reach out to your accountability partners, pastor, or other mature Christians for encouragement and prayer during difficult periods.

Remember past benefits: Keep a record of how Bible study has helped you in the past so you can refer to it during seasons when the benefits seem less obvious.

Trust the process: Understand that spiritual growth, like physical growth, isn't always immediately visible. Sometimes, Bible study is doing important work in your heart even when you don't feel it.

Integrating Bible Study with Life

Sustainable Bible study habits work best when they're integrated with the rest of your life rather than existing as a separate, isolated activity. Look for ways to connect your Bible study with other aspects of your daily routine and responsibilities.

Application-Focused Integration

Pray about what you study: Use insights from your Bible study as fuel for prayer throughout the day. If you read about God's faithfulness, thank Him for specific ways He's been faithful to you.

Share your insights: Look for natural opportunities to share what you're learning with family members, friends, or coworkers. Teaching others reinforces your own learning and creates additional accountability.

Apply principles immediately: When you discover a principle that applies to a current situation, put it into practice as soon as possible. This immediate application strengthens both your understanding and your habit.

Connect study to decisions: Use your Bible study time to seek God's wisdom for current decisions, relationships, or challenges you're facing.

Method Integration

Combine with other spiritual disciplines: Link Bible study with prayer, worship, or service to others. This integration creates a more holistic spiritual life and provides multiple reinforcements for your habits.

Use transition times: Brief moments of Scripture reading or meditation during transitions between activities can reinforce your main study time and provide spiritual focus throughout the day.

Connect to weekly worship: Choose study topics or methods that complement what your church is teaching or the sermon series your pastor is preaching.

Technology as a Tool, Not a Crutch

Modern technology offers powerful tools for Bible study, but it's important to use these tools wisely rather than depending on them to solve motivation or consistency problems.

Helpful Ways to Use Technology

Bible apps for accessibility: These apps enable you to study during previously unusable times and offer helpful features such as search, cross-references, and multiple translations.

Audio Bibles for multitasking: Listening to Scripture while commuting, exercising, or doing routine tasks can supplement your regular study time.

Digital note-taking: Apps that allow you to take notes, highlight verses, and track your reading progress can enhance your study experience.

Online study resources: Access to commentaries, dictionaries, and other study tools can enrich your understanding of difficult passages.

Potential Technology Pitfalls

Distraction: Digital devices often feature numerous distracting elements. Use technology intentionally and consider starting with physical books if digital distractions are a problem.

Passive consumption: Technology can encourage passive reading rather than active study. Make sure you're engaging thoughtfully with the text, not just consuming information.

Overwhelming options: Too many digital resources can create paralysis rather than help you study effectively. Choose a few tools and use them consistently rather than constantly switching between options.

Dependence on features: While features like reading plans and reminders can be helpful, don't depend on them entirely. Your habit should be strong enough to survive when technology fails or is unavailable.

Building Long-Term Momentum

Once you've established consistent Bible study habits, the challenge shifts from getting started to maintaining long-term growth and avoiding stagnation. Here are strategies for building momentum that sustains over months and years:

Vary Your Approach

Rotate between different types of study: Alternate between devotional reading, book studies, topical studies, and character studies to maintain interest and provide different types of spiritual nourishment.

Use different Bible translations occasionally: Reading familiar passages in different translations can provide fresh insights and prevent your study from becoming too routine.

Try different methods: The LIGHT method is excellent for building foundational habits, but don't be afraid to try other approaches as you grow in confidence and skill.

Set Progressive Goals

Increase gradually: As your habits become established, gradually increase the complexity or duration of your study time. This provides ongoing challenges without overwhelming yourself.

Add new elements: Consider adding elements like memorization, meditation, or deeper word studies to enrich your basic reading habits.

Take on special projects: Occasionally, commit to special study projects—working through a challenging book, memorizing a psalm, or studying a particular theme throughout Scripture.

Celebrate Milestones

Acknowledge consistency: Celebrate when you've maintained your habit for significant periods—30 days, 100 days, or one year.

Recognize growth: Notice and appreciate how your understanding of Scripture and your spiritual maturity have developed through consistent study.

Share your journey: Tell others about the benefits you've experienced from regular Bible study. This reinforces your own commitment and encourages others.

When Habits Need Adjustment

Even well-established habits sometimes need adjustment due to changing life circumstances, spiritual growth, or new insights about what works best for you. Don't be afraid to modify your approach when necessary.

Signs That Adjustment May Be Needed

Consistent struggle: If you find yourself constantly fighting to maintain your habit, it may be too ambitious for your current season of life.

Boredom or routine: If your Bible study feels mechanical and unrewarding despite good intentions, you may need to change your approach or method.

Life changes: Major changes in schedule, responsibilities, or living situation often require habit adjustments.

Growth in capability: As you become more skilled at Bible study, you may be ready for more challenging approaches or longer study times.

How to Adjust Wisely

Identify the specific problem: Before making changes, clearly identify what isn't working. Is the time too ambitious? Is the method too complex? Is the location inconvenient?

Make small adjustments: Change one element at a time rather than over-hauling your entire approach. This helps you identify what improvements are most helpful.

Give changes time to work: Allow several weeks to evaluate whether adjustments are helpful before making additional changes.

Maintain the core habit: Even when adjusting your approach, maintain some form of regular Bible engagement. Don't use adjustment periods as excuses to abandon study entirely.

The Role of Grace in Habit Formation

As you work to build sustainable Bible study habits, remember that God's grace is central to your spiritual growth. Your relationship with God doesn't depend on perfect consistency in Bible study, and your spiritual maturity isn't measured by how many chapters you read or how detailed your study notes are.

Grace Motivates, Not Condemns

Let God's grace motivate your Bible study rather than letting guilt drive your efforts. You study Scripture because you're loved by God and want to know Him better, not because you're trying to earn His approval or avoid His displeasure.

Progress, Not Perfection

God is patient with your growth process, and you should be patient with yourself. Focus on making progress over time rather than achieving perfect consistency immediately.

God Works Through Imperfect Efforts

Even when your Bible study feels inadequate or inconsistent, God can use it to accomplish His purposes in your life. Trust that He's working through your imperfect efforts to help you grow spiritually.

The Goal Is Relationship

Remember that the ultimate goal of Bible study habits isn't to complete a certain amount of reading or to impress others with your spiritual discipline. The goal is to know God better and grow in your relationship with Him. When this relationship is your focus, habits become a means to that end rather than an end in themselves.

Moving Forward with Confidence

Building habits that stick requires patience, realistic expectations, and practical strategies, but it's absolutely achievable for any Christian who genuinely desires to grow in their knowledge of God's Word. The key is starting where you are, not where you think you should be, and building gradually on small successes.

Don't be discouraged if your first attempts at establishing Bible study habits aren't perfect. Every mature Christian has struggled with consistency at some point. What matters isn't perfect performance from the beginning but persistent effort over time.

As you implement the strategies in this chapter, remember that you're not just building a habit—you're developing a relationship with God through His Word. This perspective transforms Bible study from a duty to be performed into a privilege to be enjoyed.

The time you invest in building sustainable Bible study habits will pay dividends throughout your Christian life. These habits will sustain you through difficult seasons, provide wisdom for important decisions, and deepen your understanding of God's character and purposes. Most importantly, they'll help you become the person God wants you to be—someone who is "throughly furnished unto all good works" (2 Timothy 3:17).

In our next chapter, we'll explore how to share what you're learning with others, which not only helps other believers grow but also reinforces your own understanding and commitment to regular Bible study.

Study Questions for Chapter 11:

1. What obstacles have prevented you from maintaining consistent Bible study habits in the past? How might the strategies in this chapter help you overcome these challenges?
2. Why is starting small more effective than setting ambitious goals when

building new habits? What would be an appropriately small starting point for your current situation?

3. How can environmental factors help or hinder habit formation? What changes could you make to your study environment to support consistency?

4. What role should accountability play in building Bible study habits? Who could you ask to provide encouragement and support in this area?

5. How can you maintain long-term momentum in Bible study without falling into mere routine or religious duty?

Practice Exercise: Design a specific, realistic Bible study habit for yourself using the principles from this chapter. Include details about when, where, and how you'll study, what your starting goal will be, and who could provide accountability. Commit to trying this approach for 30 days and evaluate your progress.

Chapter 12: Sharing What You Learn

Early on in my ministry, before I became a pastor, I discovered one of the most powerful principles of learning: we understand something best when we try to teach it to someone else. But I also found something equally important for spiritual growth: sharing what we learn from God's Word isn't just beneficial for those we teach—it's transformative for us as teachers.

Many Christians assume that sharing biblical insights is reserved for pastors, Sunday school teachers, or mature believers with seminary training. They believe they need to become experts before they can help others understand Scripture. But this assumption keeps them from experiencing one of the most effective ways to deepen their own understanding and accelerate their spiritual growth.

The truth is that you don't need to be a biblical scholar to share what you're learning from God's Word. In fact, some of the most effective teaching happens when relatively new students help others who are just a step or two behind them in the learning process. Fresh insights, recent discoveries, and the memory of what it was like to struggle with difficult concepts often make recent learners excellent teachers for those just beginning their journey.

Why Sharing Deepens Your Own Understanding

Before exploring how to share biblical insights effectively, I want you to understand why teaching others actually improves your own comprehension and retention of Scripture.

Teaching Forces Clarity

When you study the Bible for personal edification, you can get away with a vague or incomplete understanding. You might have a general sense that a passage is encouraging or convicting without being able to articulate precisely why. But when you try to explain something to another person, you're forced to think through your understanding clearly and express it in ways that others can understand.

This process of clarification often reveals gaps in your own understanding that you didn't realize existed. When you can't answer someone's question about a passage you thought you understood, you discover that your comprehension was more superficial than you realized. This discovery motivates deeper study and more careful thinking.

Teaching Requires Active Processing

Passive reading or listening allows information to pass through your mind without necessarily taking root. But teaching requires active processing—you must organize information, make connections between concepts, and find ways to make abstract truths concrete and applicable.

This active processing creates stronger neural pathways and deeper memory formation. Information you've taught to others is information you're much more likely to remember and apply in your own life.

Teaching Exposes Different Perspectives

When you share biblical insights with others, their questions and responses often reveal perspectives you hadn't considered. A child's innocent question might point out an assumption you've been making without realizing it. A skeptical friend's challenge might force you to think more carefully about why you believe what you believe.

These different perspectives don't threaten your faith—they strengthen it by helping you think more comprehensively about biblical truth and develop a more robust understanding of Scripture.

Teaching Creates Accountability

When you regularly share what you're learning from Bible study, you create natural accountability for consistent study. If your family knows you're going to share insights from your morning reading at dinner, or if your small group expects you to contribute observations about the passage you've studied, you're more motivated actually to do the study.

This accountability isn't burdensome pressure—it's a helpful structure that supports your commitment to regular Bible engagement.

Overcoming the Fear of Not Knowing Enough

The biggest obstacle most Christians face in sharing biblical insights isn't a lack of knowledge—it's fear that they don't know enough to teach others. This fear is understandable but often misplaced.

You Know More Than You Think

If you've been studying the Bible even for a short time using the methods in this book, you likely understand more than many people around you. The principles of observing context, identifying literary genres, and making careful applications put you ahead of Christians who have been reading the Bible for years without these tools.

Don't underestimate the value of basic biblical literacy. Knowing the difference between the Old and New Testaments, understanding that the Bible contains different types of literature, or being able to find a specific book of the Bible are skills that many people lack.

Teaching Doesn't Require Comprehensive Knowledge

Effective Bible teaching doesn't require you to know everything about every passage. It requires you to share accurately what you do know and to be honest about what you don't know. Some of the most helpful Bible discussions happen when someone admits they don't understand something and invites others to explore it together.

You can share a meaningful insight about God's faithfulness from Psalm 23 without being able to answer technical questions about Hebrew poetry. You can help someone understand the importance of context without needing to memorize the historical background of every biblical book.

Questions Are Opportunities, Not Threats

When people ask questions you can't answer, don't view these as exposures of your inadequacy. View them as opportunities for everyone to learn together. The response "That's a great question—I don't know the answer, but let's try to figure it out together" often leads to more meaningful learning than a comprehensive lecture.

Admitting uncertainty models intellectual humility and demonstrates that Bible study is an ongoing process of discovery rather than a test of existing knowledge.

Your Perspective Has Unique Value

Your background, experiences, and current life situation provide you with perspectives on Scripture that others may not have. A parent reading about God's love will notice things that single people might miss. Someone who has experienced financial hardship will see applications in passages about God's provision that wealthy readers might overlook.

Your unique perspective isn't a limitation—it's a contribution that enriches others' understanding of how God's Word applies to diverse life situations.

Starting Small: Family and Close Relationships

The best place to begin sharing biblical insights is with family members and close friends who already know you well and aren't expecting polished presentations. These relationships provide safe environments for developing your teaching skills without the pressure of formal educational settings.

Family Devotions and Discussions

Family devotions don't have to be elaborate, formal presentations. They can be as simple as sharing one thing you learned from your personal Bible study and asking family members what they think about it.

At the dinner table: Share a brief insight from your morning study and ask family members how they think it might apply to current family situations or decisions.

During family activities: While driving, walking, or working together, mention something from Scripture that relates to your current experience or conversation.

Bedtime conversations: End the day by sharing how something from your Bible study encouraged or challenged you, and ask family members about their own spiritual insights.

Problem-solving together: When family conflicts or decisions arise, suggest looking at relevant biblical principles together rather than just applying them unilaterally.

One-on-One Conversations

Individual conversations often provide more natural opportunities for sharing biblical insights than group settings. These conversations can happen spontaneously when friends or family members face challenges, ask spiritual questions, or express interest in what you're learning.

Listen first: Pay attention to what people are struggling with or curious about, then share relevant biblical insights rather than forcing predetermined topics into conversations.

Share personal application: Instead of lecturing about what the Bible says in general, share how specific passages have helped you deal with similar situations or questions.

Invite participation: Ask questions that help others think through biblical principles rather than just telling them what to think.

Be patient: Allow conversations to develop naturally over time rather than trying to cover everything in one discussion.

Expanding to Small Groups and Classes

As you gain confidence sharing biblical insights in family and friendship contexts, you may have opportunities to participate in or even lead small group Bible studies or Sunday school classes.

Participating Effectively in Bible Studies

Even when you're not the designated leader, you can make significant contributions to group Bible studies by sharing thoughtful observations and asking insightful questions.

Come prepared: Do your homework before group meetings. Read the passage carefully, make observations, and think about applications.

Share observations, not just applications: Many group discussions focus primarily on how passages apply to modern life without spending enough time understanding what they say. Your careful observations can help ground discussions in the text itself.

Ask clarifying questions: Help others think more carefully by asking questions like "What do you think this word means in this context?" or "How does this verse relate to what comes before it?"

Connect to broader biblical themes: Point out how the passage you're studying relates to other parts of Scripture you've learned about.

Model good discussion habits: Listen carefully to others, build on their insights, and ask follow-up questions that help everyone think more deeply.

Leading Small Group Discussions

If you're asked to lead a Bible study group, remember that your role is more about facilitating good discussion than delivering comprehensive lectures.

Prepare thoroughly but hold plans lightly: Study the passage carefully and prepare thoughtful questions, but be flexible enough to follow the Spirit's leading and the group's interests.

Ask good questions: Your most important tool as a discussion leader is questions that help people observe the text carefully and think through its implications. "What do you notice about..." and "How would you explain..."

are often more helpful than "What does this mean to you?"

Keep discussions anchored in the text: Gently redirect conversations that drift away from the actual content of the passage you're studying.

Encourage participation: Create an environment where everyone feels comfortable sharing observations and asking questions, regardless of their level of biblical knowledge.

Don't feel pressure to have all the answers: It's perfectly acceptable to say, "I don't know, but let's see if we can figure it out together" or "That's something I need to study more."

Informal Teaching Opportunities

Some of the most effective Bible teaching happens in informal contexts where people don't realize they're being "taught." These natural opportunities to share biblical insights often have a greater impact than formal presentations because they arise from real-life situations and felt needs.

Responding to Current Events

When local, national, or international events prompt spiritual questions or concerns, you can offer biblical perspectives that help others consider these situations from God's perspective.

Share relevant passages: When people express anxiety about current events, share biblical passages about God's sovereignty or peace. When they discuss moral issues, they point to relevant biblical principles.

Model biblical thinking: Demonstrate how to apply biblical principles to contemporary issues rather than just accepting cultural viewpoints uncritically.

Encourage deeper consideration: Help others move beyond surface-level reactions to events by asking questions that encourage biblical reflection.

Counseling and Encouragement

When friends, family members, or church members face difficulties, your growing understanding of Scripture equips you to offer biblical encouragement and guidance.

Listen with biblical wisdom: As you become more familiar with Scripture, you'll begin to recognize how biblical principles relate to the challenges people share with you.

Offer relevant passages: Instead of just giving advice based on your own experience or opinions, share biblical passages that address the issues people are facing.

Pray with biblical content: Use your knowledge of Scripture to inform your prayers for others, praying back God's promises and principles rather than just general requests for help.

Follow up with ongoing support: Continue to share relevant biblical insights as situations develop over time.

Sharing Through Social Media and Technology

Modern technology provides numerous platforms for sharing biblical insights with both close friends and broader audiences. These platforms require wisdom and careful consideration but can be effective tools for biblical encouragement and education.

Social Media Sharing

Share insights, not just verses: Instead of posting Bible verses without comment, share brief explanations of what you've learned from your study and how it has encouraged or challenged you.

Be authentic: Share genuinely about how Scripture is affecting your life rather than posting what you think sounds spiritual or impressive.

Encourage discussion: Ask questions that invite others to share their own insights or struggles related to the biblical principles being discussed.

Be gracious in disagreement: When people respond negatively or disagree with biblical teachings, respond with grace and humility rather than defensiveness or argumentation.

Blogging and Writing

If you enjoy writing, consider sharing your biblical insights through blogs, newsletters, or other written formats.

Focus on practical application: Write about how biblical principles have helped you navigate real-life situations rather than just providing theological commentary.

Share your learning process: Many readers appreciate honest accounts of how you've worked through difficult passages or grown in understanding over time.

Be transparent about your limitations: Acknowledge when you're sharing tentative conclusions or areas where you're still learning.

Digital Bible Study Groups

Video conferencing and messaging platforms make it possible to participate in or lead Bible studies with people who can't meet in person.

Leverage technology's advantages: Use screen sharing to review passages together, utilize digital study tools during discussions, and record sessions for those who can't attend live.

Maintain personal connection: Even in digital formats, prioritize building relationships and creating environments where people feel comfortable participating.

Making Complex Ideas Accessible

One of the most valuable skills in sharing biblical insights is the ability to make complex theological concepts understandable to people with various levels of biblical knowledge.

Use Everyday Language

Avoid theological jargon and technical terms unless you explain them clearly. Words like "sanctification," "justification," and "propitiation" may be familiar to you but meaningless to others.

Instead of saying, "This passage teaches about the believer's positional sanctification," try, "This passage explains how God sees us as holy because of what Christ has done, even though we're still growing in actual holiness."

Employ Analogies and Illustrations

Biblical concepts often become clearer when illustrated through familiar experiences or analogies.

Use contemporary examples: Explain biblical principles using modern situations that your audience can relate to—work relationships, family dynamics, current events, or common life experiences.

Draw on shared experiences: When speaking to parents, use parenting analogies to connect with them. If you're speaking to students, use school-related illustrations.

Test your analogies: Make sure your illustrations actually clarify rather than confuse the biblical concepts you're trying to explain.

Break Down Complex Ideas

Don't try to explain everything at once. Break complex theological concepts into smaller, manageable pieces that people can understand progressively.

Start with the big picture: Give people a framework for understanding before diving into details.

Build systematically: Introduce concepts in a logical order, making sure people understand each piece before moving to the next.

Check for understanding: Ask questions to ensure people are following your explanation before moving forward.

Common Mistakes to Avoid

As you begin sharing biblical insights more regularly, watch out for these common pitfalls that can hinder effective communication and damage relationships.

The Know-It-All Attitude

Avoid condescension: Don't talk down to people or make them feel foolish for not knowing things you've recently learned.

Stay humble: Remember that you're also learning and growing. Share insights with humility rather than pride.

Listen more than you speak: Show genuine interest in others' perspectives and questions rather than just waiting for your turn to talk.

The Overwhelming Information Dump

Don't share everything at once: Just because you've learned a lot doesn't mean you need to share it all in one conversation.

Focus on what's most relevant: Tailor your sharing to what people actually need or are curious about rather than what you're most excited to discuss.

Allow time for processing: Give people space to think about and respond to what you've shared before adding more information.

The Legalistic Application

Avoid being preachy: Share how biblical principles have helped you rather than telling others what they must do.

Focus on grace: Emphasize God's love and forgiveness rather than just rules and expectations.

Encourage rather than condemn: Use biblical insights to build people up rather than tear them down.

The Controversial Crusade

Choose your battles wisely: Not every biblical truth needs to be shared in every context. Use wisdom about when and how to address controversial topics.

Lead with love: Even when discussing challenging biblical teachings, emphasize God's love and your genuine care for the person you're speaking with.

Be patient with the process: Allow people time to grow in understanding rather than expecting immediate agreement or change.

Encouraging Questions and Discussions

One of the most effective ways to share biblical insights is to create environments where others feel comfortable asking questions and exploring Scripture together.

Creating Safe Spaces

Welcome all questions: Make it clear that no question is too basic, too skeptical, or too challenging. Honest questions lead to deeper understanding.

Admit your own uncertainties: Model intellectual humility by acknowledging when you don't know something or when you've changed your mind about a biblical interpretation.

Avoid quick, simplistic answers: Take time to think through complex questions rather than giving pat responses that don't really address the underlying concerns.

Focus on seeking truth together: Frame discussions as collaborative exploration rather than one-way information transfer.

Using Questions Effectively

Ask open-ended questions: Instead of questions that can be answered with yes or no, ask questions that require thought and explanation.

Follow up on responses: Build on what people say rather than just moving to the next topic. Ask, "What makes you think that?" or "Can you give an example?"

Connect to personal experience: Help people see how biblical principles relate to their own lives and circumstances.

Encourage observation: Ask questions that help people notice what the text actually says before jumping to interpretation or application.

The Ripple Effect of Sharing

When you begin sharing biblical insights regularly, you'll discover that the impact extends far beyond the immediate conversations or teaching opportunities. Your willingness to discuss Scripture creates ripple effects that benefit both you and others in unexpected ways.

Personal Growth Acceleration

Deeper study motivation: Knowing that others might ask you questions about Scripture motivates more thorough study and preparation.

Broader biblical literacy: Teaching others forces you to connect different parts of Scripture and develop a more comprehensive understanding of biblical themes.

Increased spiritual sensitivity: Regular discussion of biblical principles makes you more aware of how Scripture applies to daily life situations.

Community Building

Stronger relationships: Sharing meaningful spiritual insights often deepens relationships and creates stronger bonds with family and friends.

Mutual encouragement: When you create environments for biblical discussion, others begin sharing their insights as well, creating mutual encouragement and growth.

Church strengthening: Your participation in biblical discussions contributes to the overall spiritual health and biblical literacy of your church community.

Evangelistic Opportunities

Natural witnessing: Regular sharing of biblical insights creates natural opportunities to explain the gospel and invite others to faith in Christ.

Credible testimony: Your growing biblical knowledge gives weight to your personal testimony about what Christ has done in your life.

Apologetic preparation: Discussing Scripture with others helps you think through challenges to faith and develop thoughtful responses to skeptical questions.

Growing as a Teacher

Whether you're sharing insights informally with family members or leading formal Bible studies, you can continue growing in your ability to help others understand and apply Scripture.

Seek Feedback

Ask for honest evaluation: Request feedback from people you teach about what's most helpful and what could be improved.

Observe responses: Pay attention to how people respond to different teaching methods and adjust your approach accordingly.

Learn from experienced teachers: Watch how effective Bible teachers communicate and try to understand what makes them successful.

Continue Learning

Study teaching methods: Read books or attend workshops about effective Bible teaching and small group leadership.

Expand your biblical knowledge: Continue growing in your understanding of Scripture through systematic study, reading, and formal education opportunities.

Develop practical skills: Work on your communication skills, question-asking techniques, and group dynamics to become a more effective teacher.

Stay Connected to Purpose

Remember your motivation: Keep in mind that the goal is to help others know God better, not to impress them with your knowledge.

Focus on transformation: Measure success by spiritual growth and life change rather than just information transfer.

Depend on the Spirit: Trust that the Holy Spirit is the ultimate teacher and that your role is to be a faithful instrument in His hands.

The Joy of Shared Discovery

One of the most rewarding aspects of sharing biblical insights is experiencing the joy of shared discovery. When you help someone understand a difficult passage, see a connection they hadn't noticed before, or apply a biblical principle to their situation, you participate in the excitement of spiritual growth and learning.

This shared discovery works both ways. Often, the people you're trying to help will make observations or ask questions that deepen your own understanding. Children's innocent questions, new believers' fresh perspectives, and skeptics' challenging inquiries can all lead to insights you wouldn't have gained through individual study alone.

The process of sharing what you learn transforms Bible study from a solitary activity into a community experience. You begin to see yourself as part of the body of Christ, where each member contributes to the growth and understanding of the whole.

As the writer of Hebrews reminds us, "And let us consider one another to provoke unto love and good works: Not forsaking the assembling of ourselves together, as the manner of some is; but exhorting one another: and so much the more, as ye see the day approaching" (Hebrews 10:24-25). When you share biblical insights with others, you participate in this mutual encouragement and provocation unto good works.

Remember that you don't need to be perfect to begin sharing what you're learning. You just need to be faithful with what God has already shown you. As Jesus said in the parable of the talents, "Well done, thou good and faithful servant: thou hast been faithful over a few things, I will make thee ruler over many things: enter thou into the joy of thy lord" (Matthew 25:21).

Your faithful sharing of biblical insights, however small they may seem, contributes to God's larger purposes in building His kingdom and growing His people in spiritual maturity. The investment you make in others' biblical understanding will bear fruit not only in their lives but also in your own continued growth and development as a student and teacher of God's Word.

In our final chapters, we'll explore how to continue growing in your Bible study skills and where to find additional resources for lifelong learning.

But the foundation you've built in understanding Scripture and sharing your insights with others positions you well for a lifetime of meaningful engagement with God's Word—both for your own spiritual growth and the benefit of others in your sphere of influence.

Study Questions for Chapter 12:

1. Why does teaching others actually improve your own understanding of Scripture? Can you think of an example from your own experience where explaining something helped clarify your own thinking?

2. What fears might prevent someone from sharing biblical insights with others? How can these fears be addressed while maintaining appropriate humility?

3. What are some natural, informal opportunities in your daily life where you could share biblical insights without being preachy or forced?

4. How can you create environments where others feel comfortable asking questions about Scripture and exploring biblical truth together?

5. What's the difference between sharing biblical insights to help others grow and sharing them to demonstrate your own knowledge? How can you maintain proper motivation?

Practice Exercise: Choose one biblical insight you've gained recently from your personal study. Practice sharing this insight in three different ways: (1) a brief, informal conversation with a family member or friend, (2) a more structured explanation for someone less familiar with the Bible, and (3) a question that could spark group discussion about the topic. Notice how the process of preparing to share affects your own understanding of the insight.

V

Next Steps and Resources

Chapter 13: Where to Go from Here

Several years ago, I watched with great joy as a member of our church completed her first careful study of the Gospel of John using the LIGHT method. She had started as a complete beginner, intimidated by anything more complex than devotional reading. Still, over the course of several months, she had worked through all twenty-one chapters with growing confidence and enthusiasm.

When she finished, she came to me with a question that I had heard from many growing Bible students: "Pastor, this has been wonderful, and I feel like I'm finally starting to understand how to study the Bible properly. But now I'm not sure what to do next. Should I study another Gospel? Try one of Paul's letters? Move to the Old Testament? And should I keep using the same method, or are there other approaches I should learn? I don't want to lose the momentum I've built, but I also don't want to get stuck in a rut."

Her question reflects the exciting challenge that faces every Christian who has learned the basics of Bible study: where do you go from here? Once you've mastered fundamental skills like observation, context, and application, once you've developed consistent study habits and begun sharing insights with others, what's the next stage of your journey?

The answer isn't the same for everyone because God has made each believer unique, with different gifts, interests, and callings. But there are proven pathways for continued growth that can help you build on the foundation you've established while expanding your understanding and deepening your relationship with God through His Word.

The key is understanding that Bible study is a lifelong journey, not a destination you reach and then maintain. There will always be more to learn, deeper insights to gain, and fresh applications to discover. The goal isn't to graduate from Bible study but to continue growing in your ability to understand, apply, and share God's truth for the rest of your life.

Expanding Your Study Methods

While the LIGHT method provides an excellent foundation for Bible study, growing students benefit from learning additional approaches that can enrich their understanding and prevent their study from becoming routine or mechanical.

Topical Studies

Topical studies involve examining what the entire Bible teaches about specific subjects, such as prayer, forgiveness, God's love, spiritual warfare, or money management. This approach helps you develop a comprehensive biblical worldview on important life issues.

How to conduct topical studies: Start with a concordance to find key verses related to your topic. Use cross-references to discover additional passages. Study each passage in its context, then synthesize what you learn into a comprehensive understanding of the biblical teaching.

Benefits: Topical studies help you understand how different parts of Scripture work together to teach consistent truths. They're particularly helpful when you're facing specific life challenges or decisions that require biblical wisdom.

Potential pitfalls: Be careful not to take verses out of context just because they contain keywords related to your topic. Make sure you understand what each passage teaches in its original setting before incorporating it into your topical study.

Character Studies

Character studies focus on biblical individuals and what their lives teach us about faith, obedience, failure, and God's grace. You might study prominent figures like Abraham, Moses, and Paul or lesser-known characters like Barnabas, Lydia, or Gideon.

How to conduct character studies: Find all the passages that mention your chosen character. Study their background, major life events, relationships, strengths, weaknesses, and how God worked in their life. Look for patterns, lessons, and applications that are relevant to modern believers.

Benefits: Character studies make biblical truth concrete and personal. They show how abstract theological principles work out in real human lives, providing both encouragement and warning for contemporary believers.

Guidelines: Remember that biblical characters are human examples, not perfect models. Look for what Scripture commends or condemns about their behavior rather than assuming every action is worth imitating.

Book Studies

Studying entire books of the Bible from beginning to end helps you understand the author's complete message and see how individual passages fit into larger arguments or narratives.

How to conduct book studies: Read through the entire book several times to get the big picture. Study the book's background, including the author, audience, purpose, and historical context. Then, work through the book section by section, understanding how each part contributes to the overall message.

Benefits: Book studies prevent you from taking verses out of context and help you understand the flow of biblical thought. They also ensure you encounter the full range of biblical teaching rather than just familiar or comfortable passages.

Suggested progression: Start with shorter, clearer books, such as Philippians, 1 John, or James, before tackling longer or more complex books, like Romans, Isaiah, or Leviticus.

Word Studies

Word studies involve examining important biblical words or concepts throughout Scripture to understand their full meaning and significance.

How to conduct word studies: Choose a significant biblical word (love, faith, grace, sin, righteousness). Use a concordance to find key passages where the word appears. Study how different biblical authors use the word and how its meaning develops throughout Scripture.

Benefits: Word studies help you understand the precision and richness of biblical language. They often reveal connections between passages that use the same terminology and can clarify difficult concepts.

Tools needed: A good concordance (like Strong's) that shows you the original Hebrew or Greek words behind English translations. Some Bible software programs make word studies much easier by providing this information automatically.

Choosing Your Next Study Focus

With so many possible directions for continued Bible study, how do you decide what to tackle next? Here are some factors to consider:

Your Current Life Situation

Let your current circumstances and challenges guide some of your study choices. If you're facing financial pressure, study what the Bible says about money, work, and God's provision. If you're dealing with relationship conflicts, focus on biblical passages about forgiveness, love, and conflict resolution.

This doesn't mean your Bible study should be driven entirely by immediate needs, but allowing current situations to influence your study choices makes Scripture more immediately relevant and applicable.

Your Spiritual Growth Needs

Honestly assess areas where you need to grow spiritually and choose studies that address those needs. If you struggle with worry, study biblical passages about peace and trust. If you lack motivation for Christian living, focus on books that emphasize God's grace and the benefits of obedience.

Be honest about your weaknesses and use Bible study as a tool for addressing them systematically.

Your Biblical Knowledge Gaps

Most Christians are more familiar with some parts of the Bible than others. You might know the Gospels well but have never seriously studied the Old Testament prophets. You might be comfortable with Paul's letters but intimidated by books like Ecclesiastes or Revelation.

Identify areas of biblical illiteracy in your own knowledge and deliberately work to fill those gaps. A well-rounded biblical education requires familiarity with all types of Scripture, not just your favorites.

Your Gifts and Calling

As you grow in biblical knowledge, you may discover particular gifts for teaching, counseling, evangelism, or other ministry areas. Let these emerging gifts influence your study choices. If you have a gift for teaching children, study passages that relate to child-rearing and spiritual formation. If you sense a calling to reach unbelievers, focus on evangelistic passages and apologetic themes.

A Suggested Progression for Continued Growth

While individual needs vary, here's a general progression that works well for many growing Bible students:

Phase 1 (Months 1-6): Foundation Building

- Complete study of one Gospel (John or Mark are good starting points)
- One New Testament letter (Philippians, 1 John, or James)
- Selected Psalms using the LIGHT method
- Basic topical study on a subject of immediate interest

Phase 2 (Months 7-18): Expanding Understanding

- Study of Acts to understand early church history
- One of Paul's major letters (Romans or Ephesians)
- Character study of a prominent biblical figure
- Introduction to Old Testament narrative (Genesis or 1 Samuel)

Phase 3 (Months 19-36): Developing Depth

- Study of an Old Testament prophetic book (Isaiah 40-66 or Malachi)
- Complex New Testament book (Hebrews or Romans)
- Wisdom literature study (Proverbs or Ecclesiastes)
- Advanced topical study requiring multiple biblical sources

Phase 4 (Year 4 and beyond): Specialized Growth

- Studies based on personal calling and ministry opportunities
- Difficult books you've previously avoided
- Integration of biblical theology with practical ministry
- Teaching or mentoring others in Bible study skills

Developing Advanced Study Skills

As you grow in Bible study experience, you can develop more sophisticated skills that deepen your understanding and appreciation of Scripture.

Cross-Reference Skills

Learning to use cross-references effectively is one of the most valuable advanced skills for Bible students. Cross-references help you see how different parts of Scripture illuminate and support each other.

Types of cross-references: Verbal (exact words or phrases), conceptual (same ideas in different words), and typological (Old Testament shadows of New Testament realities).

How to use them: Don't just read cross-referenced verses in isolation. Study them in their own context first, then consider how they relate to your primary passage.

Benefits: Cross-references help you understand the unity of Scripture and prevent misinterpretation by showing how biblical authors use similar language or concepts elsewhere.

Historical and Cultural Context Skills

While you can understand much of Scripture without extensive historical knowledge, developing skills in historical and cultural contexts significantly enriches your understanding.

Basic historical framework: Learn the major periods of biblical history and how they relate to each other. Understanding the sequence of judges, kings, exile, and return helps you understand Old Testament books. Knowing the progression from Jesus' ministry through the apostolic age helps with New Testament interpretation.

Cultural awareness: Develop sensitivity to cultural differences between biblical times and today. This helps you distinguish between universal principles and culture-specific applications.

Research skills: Learn to use Bible dictionaries, atlases, and other resources to investigate historical and cultural background when it's relevant to your study.

Theological Synthesis Skills

Advanced Bible students learn to synthesize what they learn from individual passages into coherent theological understanding.

Systematic thinking: Practice organizing what you learn from various passages into a systematic understanding of major biblical themes like salvation, sanctification, or eschatology.

Progressive revelation awareness: Understand how God revealed truth gradually throughout biblical history, with later revelation building on and clarifying earlier revelation.

Doctrinal development: Learn to distinguish between core doctrines that are taught clearly throughout Scripture and secondary issues where sincere Christians may disagree.

Intermediate Study Tools

As your skills develop, you may benefit from more advanced study tools that support the deeper investigation of Scripture.

Study Bibles with Comprehensive Notes

While basic study Bibles are helpful for beginners, advanced study Bibles provide more detailed historical, cultural, and theological information that can illuminate God's Word in remarkable ways. Think of these as having a wise Bible teacher sitting right beside you as you study.

Recommended KJV Study Bibles: The Scofield Study Bible remains one of the most trusted resources for conservative Bible students. C.I. Scofield's notes have helped generations understand prophetic truth and dispensational theology. The Thompson Chain-Reference Bible (KJV) provides an incredible cross-referencing system that lets Scripture interpret Scripture—precisely what we want! For those who appreciate the beauty of the King James language with helpful study aids, the KJV Study Bible by Thomas Nelson offers solid conservative notes without compromising the majesty of the Authorized Version.

These study Bibles maintain conservative theological perspectives while providing the cultural and historical background that helps us understand what the original readers would have understood. Remember, we're not trying to make the Bible say something new—we're trying to understand what it has always said.

How to use them: Read the passage first in your regular Bible, make your own observations, and then consult the study notes for additional insight and confirmation.

Bible Software and Apps

Digital tools can significantly enhance your Bible study by providing instant access to multiple translations, original language texts, and research resources.

Popular options: Logos, Accordance, or free options like Blue Letter Bible provide access to commentaries, dictionaries, and original language tools.

Benefits: Quick word searches, cross-reference following, and comparison of multiple translations become much easier with digital tools.

Cautions: Don't let digital tools replace careful reading and thinking. Use them to enhance your study, not to shortcut the process of careful observation and interpretation.

Original Language Tools

Even without learning Greek or Hebrew, you can benefit from tools that give you access to insights from the original languages.

Interlinear Bibles: Show English text with original language words underneath, helping you see word-for-word translation choices.

Strong's Concordance: Provides a numbering system that lets you look up original language words and see how they're translated throughout Scripture.

Word study resources: Books like Vine's Expository Dictionary explain the meaning and usage of important original language words.

Avoiding Common Growth Pitfalls

As you advance in Bible study skills and knowledge, be aware of common pitfalls that can hinder your continued growth or damage your relationships with other believers.

Intellectual Pride

Knowledge can lead to pride if you're not careful. Remember that the goal of Bible study is to know God better and become more like Christ, not to impress others with your knowledge.

Signs of intellectual pride: Looking down on Christians with less biblical knowledge, using theological terms to intimidate others, or being more concerned with being right than being loving.

Prevention: Regularly remind yourself that all knowledge comes from

God, stay connected to believers who challenge your thinking, and focus on applying what you learn rather than just accumulating information.

Analysis Paralysis

Some advanced students become so focused on technical details that they lose sight of the main message and practical application of Scripture.

Signs: Spending so much time researching background information that you never get to personal application, being unable to read a passage without consulting multiple commentaries, or losing the ability to enjoy Scripture devotionally.

Prevention: Set boundaries on your research time, regularly return to simple devotional reading, and maintain focus on how passages apply to your relationship with God and others.

Theological Hobby Horses

Every growing Bible student tends to develop strong interests in particular theological topics or interpretive issues. While this can lead to valuable expertise, it can also create unhealthy obsessions.

Signs: Constantly steering conversations toward your favorite topics, evaluating everything through the lens of your particular interests, or becoming judgmental toward Christians who don't share your emphases.

Prevention: Maintain broad biblical interests, actively seek to understand different perspectives, and remember that your favorite topics may not be as important to others as they are to you.

Isolation from Community

Advanced study sometimes leads to isolation from other believers, either because you feel you've outgrown simple Bible studies or because others find your knowledge intimidating.

Prevention: Continue participating in group Bible studies even when they seem basic, practice explaining complex ideas in simple terms, and remember that teaching others often deepens your own understanding.

Setting Long-Term Learning Goals

Sustained growth in Bible study requires intentional goal-setting and planning. Without clear objectives, it's easy to drift into random reading or repetitive study of familiar passages.

Five-Year Vision

Think about where you want to be in your biblical knowledge and study skills five years from now. Do you want to have studied the entire Bible systematically? Developed expertise in particular areas? Become equipped to teach or lead Bible studies?

Having a long-term vision helps you make strategic choices about what to study and which skills to develop.

Annual Goals

Break your long-term vision into annual goals that are specific and measurable. Examples might include:

- Read through the entire Bible in a year
- Complete detailed studies of three New Testament books
- Learn to use original language tools effectively
- Teach a Bible study class or small group

Quarterly Reviews

Every three months, evaluate your progress toward your annual goals and make necessary adjustments. Life circumstances change, and your study plan should be flexible enough to adapt while maintaining forward momentum.

Weekly Planning

Each week, plan specific study activities that contribute to your larger goals. This might include which passages you'll study, what methods you'll use, or what resources you'll consult.

Finding Mentors and Learning Communities

Continued growth in Bible study is greatly enhanced by learning from others who are further along in their journey and by participating in communities of learners.

Finding Mentors

Look for mature Christians who demonstrate both biblical knowledge and godly character. Ideal mentors combine scholarly understanding with practical wisdom and spiritual maturity.

What to look for: Strong biblical knowledge, humility about their own limitations, ability to teach clearly, and demonstrated spiritual fruit in their lives.

How to approach: Be respectful of their time, come with specific questions or areas where you want to grow, and be prepared to learn from both formal teaching and informal conversation.

What to expect: Good mentors will point you to resources, answer your questions, challenge your thinking, and help you avoid common mistakes.

Learning Communities

Participate in groups of Bible students who are committed to serious study and mutual growth.

Types of communities: Seminary extension courses, church-based Bible institutes, online study groups, or informal networks of serious Bible students.

Benefits: Exposure to different perspectives, accountability for continued learning, opportunities to teach and learn from others, and support during challenging periods of study.

Choosing wisely: Look for communities that combine intellectual rigor with spiritual maturity and that welcome questions and honest discussion.

Balancing Depth and Breadth

As you advance in Bible study, you'll need to balance developing depth in particular areas with maintaining breadth across the full range of Scripture.

The Value of Breadth

A well-rounded biblical education requires familiarity with all types of Scripture—historical narrative, poetry, prophecy, epistles, and apocalyptic literature. Each genre contributes unique perspectives on God's character and purposes.

Benefits of breadth: Protection from theological imbalance, better understanding of how different parts of Scripture relate to each other, and preparation for a broader range of ministry opportunities.

Maintaining breadth: Regularly read through the entire Bible, study books from different genres, and resist the temptation to focus exclusively on your favorite types of literature.

The Value of Depth

A deep study of particular passages, books, or themes allows you to understand Scripture with greater precision and insight.

Benefits of depth: More accurate interpretation, greater appreciation for the richness of Scripture, and development of expertise that can benefit others.

Developing depth: Choose particular books or themes for extended study, use multiple methods to study the same passages, and consult various resources to gain a comprehensive understanding.

Finding Balance

Most effective Bible students develop rhythms that alternate between breadth and depth activities. You might spend six months doing a deep study of Romans, then spend the next six months reading broadly through the Old Testament historical books.

Preparing for Ministry Opportunities

As your biblical knowledge and study skills develop, you'll likely encounter opportunities to use them in service to others. Preparing for these opportunities ensures you're ready when they arise.

Teaching Preparation

If you sense God calling you toward teaching ministry, begin developing the specific skills that effective Bible teachers need.

Communication skills: Practice explaining complex ideas clearly, learn to use illustrations effectively, and develop your ability to engage audiences.

Lesson preparation: Learn to organize biblical material into coherent presentations that achieve specific learning objectives.

Classroom management: If you are teaching groups, develop skills in facilitating discussion, handling questions, and managing group dynamics.

Counseling Preparation

Many Christians with strong biblical knowledge find themselves providing informal counseling and guidance to others.

People skills: Develop your ability to listen carefully, ask good questions, and communicate empathy while maintaining biblical truth.

Wisdom application: Learn to connect biblical principles to specific life situations and practical decision-making.

Referral awareness: Understand the limits of your expertise and develop relationships with professional counselors, pastors, or other specialists for situations that require more help than you can provide.

Leadership Preparation

Biblical knowledge often opens doors to leadership opportunities in churches and other Christian organizations.

Vision development: Learn to see how biblical principles apply to organizational leadership and strategic planning.

Team building: Understand how biblical teachings about spiritual gifts, community, and service apply to building effective ministry teams.

Decision-making: Develop skills in applying biblical wisdom to complex decisions that affect groups and organizations.

Maintaining Spiritual Health in Advanced Study

As your biblical knowledge increases, it's crucial to maintain spiritual health and avoid the pitfalls that can accompany advanced learning.

Devotional Balance

Don't let analytical study completely replace devotional reading and meditation on Scripture.

Worship focus: Regularly read Scripture for the purpose of worship and adoration rather than just information gathering.

Personal application: Continue to apply what you learn to your own spiritual growth rather than just preparing to teach others.

Emotional engagement: Allow Scripture to affect your emotions, not just your intellect. The Bible should move your heart as well as inform your mind.

Community Connection

Stay connected to the broader community of believers, not just those who share your level of biblical knowledge.

Humility practice: Regularly put yourself in situations where you're learning from others rather than always being the teacher.

Service opportunities: Use your biblical knowledge in service to others rather than just for personal edification.

Accountability relationships: Maintain relationships with people who can speak into your life about pride, spiritual health, and character development.

Grace-Centered Perspective

Remember that your relationship with God depends on His grace, not your biblical knowledge.

Identity security: Find your identity in being a child of God rather than in being a Bible expert.

Gospel centrality: Keep the gospel of God's grace central to your under-standing rather than getting lost in theological details.

Love motivation: Let love for God and others motivate your study rather than desire for knowledge or recognition.

The Lifelong Journey

As you consider where to go from here in your Bible study journey, remember that this is truly a lifelong adventure. No one ever exhausts the riches of Scripture or reaches a point where they've learned everything they need to know.

This perspective should both humble and encourage you. It should humble you because it reminds you that you'll always be a student, always learning, always growing in understanding. But it should encourage you because it means the adventure never ends—there will always be fresh insights to discover, new applications to make, and a deeper appreciation for God's truth to develop.

The foundation you've built through reading this book—understanding how to observe Scripture carefully, interpret it in context, and apply it appropriately—will serve you well throughout this journey. The habits you develop and the skills you acquire will compound over time, making each year of study more productive and meaningful than the last.

Most importantly, remember that the goal isn't to become a Bible expert but to know God better and become more like Christ. Every passage you study, every insight you gain, and every application you make should contribute to this overarching purpose. When you keep this goal in focus, Bible study remains a joy rather than a burden, a relationship rather than just an academic exercise.

As Paul wrote to Timothy, "All scripture is given by inspiration of God, and is profitable for doctrine, for reproof, for correction, for instruction in righteousness: That the man of God may be perfect, throughly furnished unto all good works" (2 Timothy 3:16-17). Your continued growth in Bible study equips you not just with knowledge but also for the good works that

God has prepared for you to walk in.

The journey ahead is exciting, challenging, and deeply rewarding. With the foundation you've established and the resources available to guide your continued growth, you're well-prepared to discover the treasures that await you in God's Word. The question isn't whether you're ready for the journey— it's whether you're ready to take the next step.

Study Questions for Chapter 13:

1. Based on your current Bible study experience and spiritual growth needs, which type of study (topical, character, book, or word study) would be most beneficial for you to try next?

2. What factors should guide your decisions about what to study as you continue growing? How can you balance personal interests with areas where you need to grow?

3. What are some potential pitfalls that could hinder your continued growth in Bible study? How can you guard against these dangers?

4. How can you maintain the balance between gaining biblical knowledge and applying it practically to your spiritual life and relationships?

5. What long-term goals do you have for your Bible study journey? How can you break these into manageable steps for continued progress?

Practice Exercise: Create a personalized plan for the next six months of Bible study. Choose what you'll study, which methods you'll use, what resources you might need, and how you'll measure your progress. Be specific but realistic, and build on the foundation you've already established rather than starting completely over.

Chapter 14: Building Your Study Library

The right resources can dramatically accelerate your Bible study growth, helping you understand difficult passages, providing crucial background information, and exposing you to insights from mature believers throughout church history. But the wrong resources—or even good resources used poorly—can overwhelm you with information, create dependence on human opinions rather than careful study, or lead you into theological confusion.

The goal isn't to accumulate an impressive collection of books but to carefully select resources that actually enhance your understanding of Scripture and support your spiritual growth. This chapter will help you make wise choices about which study tools to acquire, how to evaluate their quality and usefulness, and how to use them effectively without becoming overly dependent on them.

Principles for Building a Study Library

Before we examine specific types of resources, let's establish some foundational principles that should guide your decisions about what to include in your study library.

Start with Needs, Not Wants

The most common mistake people make when building a study library is buying resources based on what seems impressive or comprehensive rather than what they actually need for their current level of study. A beginning Bible student doesn't need a 50-volume commentary set or advanced tools in original languages.

Instead, identify specific needs in your Bible study and find resources that address those needs. Do you struggle with understanding historical context? Get a good Bible dictionary. Are you confused by difficult words or concepts? Start with a basic Bible handbook. Do you want to understand how different parts of Scripture relate to each other? Invest in a study Bible with good cross-references.

Quality Over Quantity

It's better to own five excellent resources that you use regularly than fifty mediocre ones that gather dust on your shelf. Focus on acquiring high-quality tools from trusted authors rather than trying to build an extensive library quickly.

High-quality resources will serve you well for many years, providing reliable information you can trust. Poor-quality resources can actually hinder your Bible study by providing inaccurate information or leading you toward theological confusion.

Build Gradually

Don't try to assemble a complete study library all at once. Build gradually, adding resources as your skills develop and your needs become clearer. What seems essential to an advanced student might be overwhelming or unnecessary for a beginner.

Begin with basic tools and gradually add more specialized resources as you gain experience and identify areas where you require additional assistance. This approach allows you to learn how to use each resource effectively before adding new ones.

Maintain Biblical Authority

Remember that your study library should support your understanding of Scripture, not replace it. The Bible is your ultimate authority, and all other resources are simply tools to help you understand what God has already revealed in His Word.

Don't let commentaries, study notes, or other resources become crutches that prevent you from doing your own careful reading and thinking. Use them to enhance your study, not to shortcut the process of careful observation and interpretation.

Consider Your Budget

Building a sound study library doesn't require a large budget. Still, it does require wisdom in allocating your resources. Set a realistic budget for study materials and prioritize your purchases based on your actual needs rather than what you think you should own.

Many excellent resources are available at reasonable prices, and some of the best study tools are completely free. Don't assume that expensive equals better, and don't go into debt to build a study library.

Essential Resources for Every Bible Student

Regardless of your level of experience or particular interests, certain types of resources are valuable for virtually every serious Bible student. These form the foundation of a sound study library.

A Reliable Primary Bible

Your most important resource is a good Bible that you can mark, underline, and use for daily study. While digital Bibles are convenient for many purposes, having a physical Bible for primary study offers advantages that digital versions can't match.

Why the King James Version?

As we discussed in Chapter 2, the King James Version offers several advantages that make it an excellent choice for serious Bible study. Its manuscript foundation, translation precision, and historical stability provide a reliable foundation for study. The slightly formal language, while challenging at first, actually enhances your understanding of Scripture's dignity and significance.

Choosing a study edition: Look for a KJV with good cross-references, maps, and basic study helps. The Scofield Reference Bible and the Thompson Chain Reference Bible are excellent options that provide helpful study features without overwhelming readers with excessive notes.

Binding and format: Choose a binding that will withstand regular use. Genuine leather or high-quality bonded leather typically lasts longer than paperback or hardcover bindings. Consider the size—large enough to read comfortably but portable enough to carry regularly.

A Comprehensive Concordance

A concordance is an alphabetical index of the words used in the Bible, showing you every place each word appears. For serious Bible study, a concordance is indispensable.

Strong's Exhaustive Concordance is the gold standard for KJV users. It lists every word in the KJV and provides numbers that correspond to the original Hebrew and Greek words. This allows you to study the meaning of biblical words even without knowing the original languages.

How to use a concordance: Look up any significant word from your passage to see how it's used elsewhere in Scripture. This helps you understand the word's full biblical meaning and see connections between different passages.

Benefits: Concordances help you let Scripture interpret Scripture, find parallel passages, and study biblical themes comprehensively.

A Quality Bible Dictionary

A Bible dictionary explains the people, places, customs, and concepts mentioned in Scripture. It provides the historical and cultural background information that's often essential for understanding biblical passages.

Recommended options: Easton's Bible Dictionary, Smith's Bible Dictionary, or the New Bible Dictionary provide reliable information from conservative perspectives. These dictionaries explain everything from biblical weights and measures to theological concepts.

How to use: When you encounter unfamiliar names, places, or customs in your Bible reading, look them up in your Bible dictionary. This background information often clarifies passages that seem confusing or irrelevant.

A Reliable Bible Commentary

A good commentary provides verse-by-verse explanations of Scripture written by careful scholars. However, choosing the right commentary requires wisdom because not all commentaries are equally reliable or helpful.

For beginners: Matthew Henry's Commentary on the Whole Bible is a classic that combines careful exegesis with practical application. While written in an older style, it provides reliable interpretation from a thoroughly biblical perspective. Another excellent resource for beginners is Willmington's Guide to the Bible.

For intermediate students: John Phillips' Exploring Commentary series provides thorough, verse-by-verse exposition from a dispensational perspective. Oliver B. Greene's commentary series offers practical, soul-winning focused interpretations that emphasize personal application. For those seeking more academic depth, John Walvoord and Roy Zuck's Bible Knowledge Commentary provides scholarly analysis from a conservative, premillennial viewpoint that aligns well with Baptist theological positions.

How to use commentaries: Always study the passage yourself first, then consult commentaries to check your understanding and gain additional insights. Don't let commentaries do your thinking for you.

Intermediate Resources for Growing Students

As your Bible study skills develop and your knowledge increases, additional resources can provide deeper insights and more specialized help.

Multiple Bible Translations

While the KJV should remain your primary study Bible, comparing different translations can sometimes clarify difficult passages or reveal nuances you might miss with just one translation.

Useful comparisons: The New King James Version updates archaic language while maintaining the KJV's translation philosophy. The English Standard Version and New American Standard Bible provide more literal translations that can help clarify difficult passages.

How to use: When studying a challenging passage, read it in several reliable translations to see how different scholars have understood the original text. Look for common elements that appear in all translations—these are likely to reflect the clear meaning of the original.

Caution: Don't use translation comparison as an excuse to choose whichever version says what you want it to say. The goal is to understand the truth, not to find support for predetermined conclusions.

Bible Atlases and Maps

Understanding the geography of biblical events often clarifies passages that seem confusing without this context. A good Bible atlas illustrates the locations where biblical events took place and helps you understand the movement of people and armies throughout biblical history.

What to look for: Clear, accurate maps that cover all major biblical periods, explanations of how geography affected historical events, and photographs of important biblical sites.

How to use: When studying historical narratives, locate the events on your maps. Understanding distances, terrain, and political boundaries often explain why certain events unfolded as they did.

Topical Bibles

A topical Bible organizes Scripture verses by subject, making it easy to study what the Bible teaches about specific topics, such as prayer, forgiveness, money, or spiritual warfare.

Popular options: Nave's Topical Bible or Thompson's Topical Chain Reference Bible provide comprehensive listings of verses related to hundreds of topics.

How to use: When you want to study a particular subject, use a topical Bible to find relevant passages throughout Scripture. Study each passage in its context before concluding what the Bible teaches on that topic.

Benefits: Topical Bibles help you develop comprehensive biblical perspectives on important life issues and see how different parts of Scripture address the same themes.

Church History Resources

Understanding how Christians throughout history have interpreted and applied Scripture can provide valuable perspective on your own study.

Basic church history: Books like "The Trail of Blood" by J.M. Carroll provides an honest perspective on church history, tracing what the author sees as the succession of New Testament churches through various groups who maintained biblical practices despite persecution. "A History of the Baptists" by John T. Christian offers a comprehensive overview of Baptist heritage and principles from a distinctly Baptist viewpoint. For those seeking broader context while maintaining conservative perspectives, "Church History" by Earle E. Cairns provides an evangelical overview of Christian history.

Historical theology: Resources that explain how major doctrines developed throughout church history help you understand why certain interpretations became widely accepted.

Benefits: Church history resources help you avoid interpretive errors that have been identified and corrected in the past, and they connect you with the wisdom of mature believers from previous generations.

Advanced Resources for Serious Students

As you become more skilled in Bible study and develop particular interests or calling in ministry areas, more specialized resources can provide deeper insights and technical information.

Original Language Tools

Even without learning Greek and Hebrew, you can benefit from tools that give you access to insights from the original languages.

Interlinear Bibles: Show the English text with the original language words underneath, helping you see word-for-word translation choices and understand the structure of the original text.

Lexicons and dictionaries: Resources like Vine's Expository Dictionary or Thayer's Greek-English Lexicon explain the meaning and usage of original language words.

Word study books: Books that focus on important biblical words and concepts, explaining their meaning and usage throughout Scripture.

How to use: When studying keywords or complex concepts, use these tools to understand how the original language words were used and what they meant to the original audience.

Specialized Commentaries

As your interests develop, you may want commentaries that focus on particular books of the Bible or provide more technical analysis.

Expositional commentaries: Provide detailed verse-by-verse explanations of specific books. Look for authors known for careful scholarship and biblical faithfulness.

Technical commentaries: Provide detailed analysis of original languages, textual variants, and scholarly debates. These are most useful for advanced students who want to understand interpretive options for difficult passages.

Devotional commentaries: Focus more on practical application and spiritual insights than technical analysis. These can enrich your personal study even when you're using other resources for detailed analysis.

Reference Works

Advanced students often benefit from comprehensive reference works that provide detailed information on biblical and theological topics.

Bible encyclopedias: Multi-volume works that provide extensive articles on biblical topics, people, places, and concepts.

Theological dictionaries: Explain important theological terms and concepts with detailed analysis and biblical support.

Biblical archaeology resources: Provide information about archaeological discoveries that shed light on biblical history and culture.

Digital Resources and Technology

Modern technology offers access to vast libraries of biblical resources, often at a significantly lower cost than print versions. However, using digital resources effectively requires wisdom and discipline.

Bible Software

Comprehensive Bible software programs offer access to multiple translations, commentaries, dictionaries, and other resources in a single, integrated package.

Popular options: Logos Bible Software, Accordance, or BibleWorks provide professional-level tools for serious Bible study. Free options, such as e-Sword or Blue Letter Bible, offer basic functionality at no cost.

Benefits: Instant word searches, cross-reference following, comparison of multiple resources, and access to resources that would be expensive to purchase individually.

Considerations: Learning to use sophisticated software effectively takes time and effort. Don't let the technology become more important than the actual Bible study.

Online Resources

Numerous websites provide free access to study tools, commentaries, and reference works.

Reliable sites: Blue Letter Bible, Bible Gateway, and Bible Hub provide access to multiple translations, commentaries, and study tools. Sites affiliated with solid seminaries or established ministries typically offer reliable information.

Free classics: Many classic commentaries and reference works are available free online through sites like Christian Classics Ethereal Library or Archive.org.

Caution: Evaluate online resources carefully. The internet contains both excellent and terrible biblical resources, and it's not always easy to distinguish between them.

Mobile Apps

Bible apps allow you to study during previously unusable times and provide convenient access to study tools.

Popular options: YouVersion, Olive Tree, or Logos mobile apps provide access to multiple translations and study resources on smartphones and tablets.

Benefits: Study during commutes, lunch breaks, or waiting periods. Offline access to resources when the internet isn't available.

Limitations: Small screens can make detailed study difficult, and the convenience can sometimes lead to superficial rather than careful study.

Evaluating Resource Quality

With so many study resources available, how do you evaluate their quality and usefulness? Here are key criteria to consider:

Theological Perspective

Choose resources written from a perspective that aligns with your under-standing of biblical authority and essential Christian doctrines.

Conservative evangelical authors typically affirm biblical inerrancy, salvation by grace through faith, and other fundamental Christian doctrines. This doesn't mean you can't learn from authors with different perspectives, but it's helpful to understand their theological framework.

Red flags: Be cautious about resources that question biblical authority, deny essential Christian doctrines, or promote views that clearly contradict Scripture.

Scholarly Credentials

While academic credentials aren't everything, they can indicate whether an author has the knowledge and training necessary to write reliable biblical resources.

What to look for: Authors with degrees from accredited seminaries or biblical studies programs, demonstrated knowledge of original languages, and recognition within evangelical scholarship.

Balance: Remember that some of the most helpful resources are written by pastors and teachers who combine scholarly knowledge with practical ministry experience.

Practical Usefulness

The best resources are those you'll actually use regularly in your Bible study.

Clarity: Choose resources written in a language you can understand. Overly technical works aren't helpful if you can't comprehend them.

Organization: Well-organized resources featuring good indexes, cross-references, and navigation features are significantly more helpful than those that are poorly organized.

Relevance: Choose resources that address your actual needs and interests rather than trying to impress others with comprehensive coverage.

Reputation and Reviews

Resources that have been helpful to other serious Bible students are likely to be helpful to you as well.

Longevity: Resources that have remained in print and popular for many years have usually proven their value over time.

Recommendations: Ask pastors, mature Christians, or Bible study teachers which resources they've found most helpful.

Reviews: Read reviews from multiple sources, paying attention to both positive and negative feedback.

Using Your Library Effectively

Having good resources is only half the battle—you need to use them effectively to benefit from your investment.

Develop a System

Organization: Keep your resources organized so you can quickly find what you need. This might mean arranging books by type, topic, or frequency of use.

Note-taking: Develop a system for recording insights you gain from your study resources. This might be marginal notes in your Bible, a separate notebook, or digital notes.

Cross-referencing: Note connections between different resources and passages to easily find related information.

Maintain Proper Priorities

Bible first: Always study the biblical text first before consulting other resources. Let Scripture be your primary authority, and use other resources to enhance your understanding.

Multiple sources: Don't rely on just one commentary or resource. Compare insights from different sources and let Scripture serve as the arbiter when they disagree.

Personal reflection: Don't let resources do all your thinking for you. Take time to reflect on what you've learned and how it applies to your life.

Avoid Common Pitfalls

Information overload: Don't try to consult every available resource for every passage you study. Choose a few reliable resources and use them consistently.

Paralysis by analysis: Don't let research prevent you from applying what you learn. At some point, you need to move from study to application.

Academic pride: Don't use your resources to show off your knowledge or to win arguments. Use them to understand the truth and cultivate your spiritual growth.

Building on a Budget

You don't need a large budget to build an effective study library. Here are strategies for acquiring good resources without overspending:

Prioritize Essentials

Start with the basic resources that will serve you well across all your

Bible study: a good Bible, a concordance, a Bible dictionary, and a basic commentary. Add specialized resources only after you've mastered these fundamentals.

Buy Used

Many excellent study resources are available used at significant savings. Check:

- Used bookstores, especially those that specialize in religious books
- Online marketplaces like Amazon, eBay, or AbeBooks
- Church libraries that are updating their collections
- Seminary bookstores that sell used textbooks

Take Advantage of Sales

- Many publishers offer significant discounts during holiday seasons
- Seminary bookstores often have sales when updating inventory
- Digital resources frequently go on sale for much less than print versions

Use Free Resources

- Many classic commentaries and reference works are available free online
- Public libraries often have good biblical resources
- Some churches have lending libraries available to members
- Free Bible software and apps provide access to many study tools

Share Resources

- Consider sharing the cost of expensive resources with other serious Bible students.
- Some study groups purchase resources collectively for shared use
- Seminary libraries often allow community members to use their resources

Growing Your Library Over Time

Your study library should grow and evolve as your knowledge and interests develop. Here's how to plan for long-term growth:

Regular Evaluation
Periodically evaluate your current resources:

- Which ones do you use regularly?
- Which ones have proven most helpful?
- What gaps exist in your current collection?
- What new needs have developed as your study skills have grown?

Strategic Additions
Rather than buying randomly, make strategic additions based on the following:

- Areas where you're doing focused study
- Ministry opportunities that require specialized knowledge
- Gaps in your current collection that hinder your study
- Recommendations from teachers or mentors whose judgment you trust

Quality Upgrades
As your budget allows, consider upgrading basic resources with higher-quality versions:

- Replace paperback Bibles with durable leather editions
- Upgrade to more comprehensive commentaries as your skills develop
- Add specialized resources that address your particular interests or calling

Format Considerations
Think carefully about whether to add resources in print or digital format:

- Print books are often easier to browse and annotate
- Digital resources are searchable and portable
- Some resources work better in one format than another
- Your personal study habits may favor one format over another

Your Library as a Ministry Tool

As your study library grows and your biblical knowledge increases, your resources become tools not just for your own growth but for serving others.

Teaching Preparation

Good resources help you prepare to teach others more effectively:

- Commentaries provide insights you can share with students
- Historical resources help you explain the background of biblical events
- Reference works help you answer questions that arise during teaching

Counseling and Encouragement

Biblical resources equip you to provide better guidance and encouragement to others:

- Topical resources help you find relevant passages for specific problems
- Character studies provide examples of how biblical figures dealt with similar challenges
- Devotional resources offer insights for personal encouragement

Apologetics and Evangelism

Study resources help you defend the faith and explain the gospel more effectively:

- Reference works help you answer questions about apparent contradictions or difficult passages
- Historical resources demonstrate Christianity's intellectual credibility

· Commentaries help you understand and explain complex theological concepts

The Ultimate Goal

Remember that the ultimate goal of building a study library isn't to accumulate impressive resources or to become a biblical expert. The goal is to know God better and to become more effective in serving Him and others.

Your study library should serve your relationship with God, not replace it. Resources should enhance your understanding of Scripture, not replace careful personal study. The best library in the world is worthless if it doesn't help you love God more deeply and serve Him more faithfully.

As you build your study library, keep in mind Paul's words to Timothy: "All scripture is given by inspiration of God, and is profitable for doctrine, for reproof, for correction, for instruction in righteousness: That the man of God may be perfect, throughly furnished unto all good works" (2 Timothy 3:16-17).

Your study resources should help you become "throughly furnished unto all good works"—equipped not just with knowledge but with practical wisdom for living and serving according to God's will. When your library serves this purpose, it becomes a valuable investment in your spiritual growth and your ability to serve others effectively.

The foundation you've built through the principles and methods in this book, combined with carefully chosen study resources, positions you well for a lifetime of meaningful Bible study. As you continue to grow in your understanding of God's Word and your ability to apply it to life, you'll discover that the journey of biblical learning is one of the most rewarding adventures you can undertake.

Whether your library consists of a few essential resources or expands to include more specialized tools, the key is to utilize whatever resources you have to gain a deeper understanding and apply God's truth. Start with what you can afford, build gradually, and let your growing understanding of Scripture guide your choices about what to add next.

The goal isn't to own every possible study resource but to carefully select tools that actually enhance your understanding of God's Word and support your spiritual growth. When you approach library building with this perspective, you'll find that even a modest collection of well-chosen resources can significantly enrich your Bible study and accelerate your spiritual development.

Study Questions for Chapter 14:

1. What principles should guide your decisions about which study resources to acquire? How can you avoid the common mistake of accumulating impressive resources you don't actually use?

2. Why is it important to maintain the Bible's authority while using study resources? How can you use commentaries and other tools to enhance rather than replace your own careful study?

3. What are the essential resources that every serious Bible student should consider acquiring? How do these basic tools support the study methods you've learned in this book?

4. How should your budget constraints affect your approach to building a study library? What strategies can help you acquire good resources without overspending?

5. How can your study library become a tool for serving and teaching others, not just for your own growth?

Practice Exercise: Evaluate your current study resources and create a plan for building your library over the next year. Identify what essential resources you already have, what gaps exist in your collection, and what your next priority should be based on your current study needs and budget. Research specific resources that meet your identified needs and compare options before making decisions.

Conclusion: You Can Do This

Do you remember how this journey began? You picked up this book because the Bible seemed overwhelming, intimidating, or simply too difficult to understand on your own. Maybe you'd tried to read through Scripture before and gotten bogged down in genealogies or confused by cultural references you didn't understand. Perhaps you'd attended Bible studies where everyone else seemed to grasp insights that completely escaped you.

If you felt lost, confused, or inadequate when you started reading this book, you weren't alone. Every mature Christian has been precisely where you were—staring at God's Word with a genuine desire to understand but feeling overwhelmed by the task. The Ethiopian eunuch, reading Isaiah in his chariot, spoke for countless believers throughout history when he asked, "How can I, except some man should guide me?" (Acts 8:31).

But look how far you've come.

You now understand what the Bible is—not a collection of random religious writings, but God's unified revelation of His character and His plan of redemption through Jesus Christ. You know that this incredible book, written by dozens of authors over fifteen centuries, tells one coherent story because it has one ultimate Author.

You've learned to distinguish between what Scripture says and what it means, understanding that careful observation must precede accurate interpretation. You know that context is king and that different types of biblical literature require different reading approaches. That apparent contradictions often resolve when examined carefully with proper tools and perspective.

You've discovered practical methods, such as the LIGHT approach, that transform Bible reading from overwhelming confusion into systematic understanding. You've learned to make Scripture personal without making it all about you, understanding that God's Word was written for you, not to you, and that proper application flows from proper interpretation.

Most importantly, you've begun to see Bible study not as an academic exercise but as a pathway to a deeper relationship with God. You understand that the goal isn't to master Scripture but to be mastered by it; not to accumulate biblical knowledge, but to be transformed by biblical truth.

The Journey You've Traveled

Let's take a moment to appreciate the distance you've covered. When you started this book, you may have felt like that discouraged church member I mentioned in the introduction—wondering if you were smart enough, spiritual enough, or equipped enough to understand God's Word.

Now you have practical tools for Bible study that work. You understand how to:

Read Scripture carefully and purposefully, looking for what God actually said rather than what you hoped He said or what you assumed He meant.

Interpret passages in their proper context, understanding what they meant to their original audience before determining how they apply to your life today.

Handle difficult passages and apparent contradictions without losing confidence in Scripture's reliability, knowing that most challenges have reasonable explanations when examined carefully.

Apply biblical principles appropriately to your modern circumstances, distinguishing between universal truths and culturally specific applications.

Build sustainable study habits that can weather the storms of busy schedules, changing circumstances, and inevitable periods of spiritual dryness.

Share your insights with others in ways that encourage spiritual growth and biblical understanding in your family, friends, and church community.

You've also learned to avoid common pitfalls that derail many Bible students: proof-texting verses out of context, making everything about your personal circumstances, getting overwhelmed by information rather than focusing on transformation, and depending on study resources rather than developing your own careful reading skills.

Perhaps most significantly, you've discovered that confusion about Scripture doesn't indicate failure—it means the beginning of learning. Every difficult passage you encounter is an opportunity to grow in understanding. Every question that arises during your study is a doorway to deeper insight. Every challenge to your interpretation is a chance to examine Scripture more carefully and think more precisely about what God has revealed.

What You've Really Learned

The specific methods and tools you've mastered are valuable, but they're not the most important things you've gained from this journey. The real treasure is the confidence and competence you've developed—the quiet assurance that you can approach God's Word with expectation rather than intimidation.

You've learned to trust Scripture's reliability even when you don't understand everything perfectly. You know that God's Word has proven itself trustworthy for centuries and that apparent difficulties usually reflect limitations in your knowledge rather than errors in the text.

You've learned to trust your ability to understand Scripture when you apply sound principles of interpretation. You're not dependent on others to tell you what the Bible means—you can read it carefully, think about it clearly, and apply it appropriately to your own life.

You've learned to trust the Holy Spirit's guidance as you study, knowing that the same Spirit who inspired Scripture is present to illuminate it for believers who approach it with humble, teachable hearts.

You've learned to trust the process of gradual growth in understanding. You don't expect to master difficult passages immediately. Still, you're confident that consistent, careful study will deepen your comprehension over time.

Most importantly, you've learned that Bible study isn't about becoming a religious expert but about knowing God more intimately. Every insight you gain, every principle you apply, and every truth you share contributes to the overarching purpose of Christian life: being "conformed to the image of his Son" (Romans 8:29).

The Adventure Continues

Completing this book doesn't mark the end of your Bible study journey—it marks the beginning of a lifelong adventure in God's Word. You now have the tools and confidence you need to explore Scripture with growing effectiveness and deepening appreciation.

The Bible's Inexhaustible Riches

Even after decades of careful study, you'll continue to discover new insights, fresh applications, and a deeper appreciation for God's truth. The Bible's richness is inexhaustible because it reveals an infinite God who finite minds cannot fully comprehend.

This means you'll never outgrow the wonder of Bible study. The same passage that encouraged you as a new believer will speak to you in new ways as you face different circumstances and grow in spiritual maturity. God's Word has layers of meaning and application that can supply fresh insights throughout your entire Christian journey.

Your Growing Influence

As your biblical knowledge and study skills continue developing, you'll discover increasing opportunities to influence others for good. Your family members will benefit from your growing biblical wisdom. Your friends will seek your counsel because they trust your understanding of Scripture. Your church will find ways to use your gifts in teaching, mentoring, or serving.

Don't underestimate the ripple effects of your faithful Bible study. When you understand God's Word clearly and apply it consistently, you become a conduit of biblical truth that can impact countless other lives. The insights you share, the example you set, and the wisdom you offer all contribute to the spiritual growth of your community.

Your Deepening Relationship with God

Most significantly, your continued Bible study will deepen your relationship with God in ways you can't yet imagine. Each new understanding of His character draws you closer to Him. Each fresh appreciation of His grace increases your love for Him. Each deeper grasp of His purposes strengthens your trust in Him.

The God you know today through His Word is the same God you'll know more intimately tomorrow as you continue studying. Your relationship with Him will grow richer, deeper, and more satisfying as you spend time in His Word consistently over the years ahead.

Practical Next Steps

As you close this book and continue your Bible study journey, here are some practical suggestions for maintaining momentum and continuing growth:

Maintain Your Study Habits

The habits you've developed while reading this book are precious assets. Protect them carefully. Continue using the LIGHT method or other approaches you've found helpful. Maintain your study schedule even when motivation wanes. Remember that consistency matters more than intensity in building long-term spiritual growth.

Continue Building Your Library

Add study resources gradually as your needs become clearer, and your budget allows. Focus on quality rather than quantity, choosing resources that will actually enhance your understanding rather than impress your friends.

Seek Ongoing Learning Opportunities

Look for Bible study groups, Sunday school classes, or other learning opportunities that challenge you to grow. Consider taking courses at a local Bible college or seminary if such opportunities are available. Read books by mature Bible teachers who can expand your understanding and sharpen your skills.

Find Teaching Opportunities

Look for ways to share what you're learning with others. This might involve teaching a Sunday school class, leading a small group Bible study, mentoring a newer believer, or simply being more intentional about discussing Scripture with family and friends.

Stay Connected to Your Purpose

Remember that the goal of Bible study is to foster a deeper relationship with God, not just to accumulate knowledge. Regular times of worship, prayer, and reflection help maintain a proper perspective on your study efforts. Let your growing understanding of Scripture fuel a more profound love for God and more faithful service to others.

When Challenges Come

Your Bible study journey won't always be smooth sailing. You'll encounter periods of dryness when Scripture seems routine or uninteresting. You'll face challenging life circumstances that make it difficult to concentrate on your studies. You'll wrestle with passages that remain confusing despite your best efforts to understand them.

During these challenging seasons, remember the foundation you've built. The principles you've learned don't become invalid when you feel discouraged. The methods you've mastered don't stop working when life gets complicated. The God who speaks through His Word doesn't become silent when you feel spiritually dry.

Persist Through Dryness

Spiritual dryness is a normal part of every believer's journey. When Bible study feels mechanical or unrewarding, don't abandon it—adjust it. Perhaps focus on passages that have encouraged you in the past. Maybe try a different study method or approach. Consider studying with others who can provide fresh perspectives and mutual encouragement.

Remember that faithfulness during dry seasons often produces the deepest spiritual growth. When you study Scripture not because you feel like it but because you're committed to knowing God better, you demonstrate the kind of mature devotion that pleases Him.

Learn from Difficulties

When you encounter passages or concepts that remain confusing despite careful study, use these difficulties as opportunities for growth. Research the background more thoroughly. Consult additional resources. Discuss your questions with mature believers. Sometimes, understanding comes gradually through persistent effort rather than immediate insight.

Don't let unanswered questions shake your confidence in Scripture's reliability. Remember that the essential truths of Christianity are taught clearly throughout the Bible. Secondary issues may remain unclear, but the central message of God's love, Christ's salvation, and the Christian life is crystal clear.

Trust God's Timing

Sometimes, God reveals truth according to His timeline rather than yours. A passage that seems incomprehensible today may become clear when you face circumstances that require exactly that truth. A principle that seems abstract in youth may become profoundly practical in middle age. Trust that God will provide the understanding you need when you need it.

Your Responsibility and Privilege

As we conclude this journey together, it's important to acknowledge both the responsibility and the privilege that come with understanding God's Word.

The Responsibility

"For unto whomsoever much is given, of him shall be much required" (Luke 12:48). The biblical knowledge and study skills you've developed carry with them the responsibility to use them faithfully.

You're responsible for continuing to grow in your understanding rather than becoming complacent with what you've already learned. You're accountable for applying biblical truth to your own life rather than just accumulating knowledge for its own sake. You're responsible for sharing your insights with others rather than hoarding them for yourself.

Most importantly, you're responsible for allowing Scripture to transform your character rather than inform your mind. The goal isn't to become a biblical expert but to become more like Christ.

The Privilege

At the same time, never lose sight of the incredible privilege you enjoy. Throughout most of human history, ordinary people didn't have access to God's written Word. They couldn't read it in their own language, study it with helpful resources, or discuss it freely with other believers.

You live in an era of unprecedented access to Scripture and biblical resources. You can carry God's Word with you wherever you go. You can study it in multiple translations, with extensive commentary, and with tools that make the original languages accessible even to non-scholars.

This privilege comes from God's grace and the sacrificial efforts of countless believers throughout history who preserved, copied, translated, and defended Scripture so that you could have access to it today. Don't take this privilege lightly.

God's Word Will Accomplish Its Purpose

As you continue your Bible study journey, remember God's promise through the prophet Isaiah: "So shall my word be that goeth forth out of my mouth: it shall not return unto me void, but it shall accomplish that which I please, and it shall prosper in the thing whereto I sent it" (Isaiah 55:11).

God's Word will accomplish its purpose in your life. Every moment you spend studying Scripture, every insight you gain, every truth you apply contributes to God's work of conforming you to Christ's image. Even when you feel like you're not learning much or growing fast enough, God is using His Word to accomplish His purposes in ways you may not immediately recognize.

Trust the process. Trust God's Word. Trust His plan for your spiritual development. The time you invest in Bible study is never wasted, even when the results aren't immediately apparent.

A Personal Promise

Let me close with a personal promise, based on more than twenty years of watching Christians grow through faithful Bible study: if you continue to apply the principles and methods you've learned in this book, your relationship with God will deepen in ways you cannot currently imagine.

Five years from now, you'll look back on your current level of biblical understanding the way you now look back on where you were when you started reading this book. You'll be amazed at how much you've learned, how much your perspective has matured, and how much more intimate your relationship with God has become.

Ten years from now, you'll be helping other believers discover the same joy and confidence in Bible study that you've experienced. You'll share insights that encourage the discouraged, provide wisdom that guides the confused, and demonstrate that anyone can truly understand God's Word when they approach it with the right tools and perspective.

The Ethiopian's Joy

Remember the Ethiopian eunuch we met in the introduction? After Philip explained the Scriptures to him, the eunuch responded with joy and faith, requesting immediate baptism. When he continued his journey, he went "on his way rejoicing" (Acts 8:39).

That's the picture of where you are now. You've had the Scriptures explained to you through this book. You've discovered that God's Word is not only understandable, accessible, and transformative but also a powerful source of guidance and inspiration. You've learned that you don't need to be a scholar or a pastor to understand what God has revealed.

Now, you can go on your way rejoicing, confident that you have the tools and understanding you need to continue growing in your knowledge of God through His Word. The confusion and intimidation you felt when you started this journey have been replaced by confidence and competence.

You've discovered the truth that Philip helped the Ethiopian understand: God's Word is meant for ordinary people who hunger to know Him better. The Bible isn't a mysterious book reserved for religious professionals—it's God's revelation to anyone who approaches it with a sincere heart and sound principles of interpretation.

You Can Do This

The title of this conclusion isn't just encouragement—it's a statement of fact. You can do this. You can understand God's Word. You can apply it to your life. You can share it with others. You can continue growing in biblical knowledge and spiritual maturity throughout your life.

You've already proven you can do this by working through this book and applying its principles to your own Bible study. The foundation you've built is solid, the tools you've acquired are reliable, and the confidence you've developed is well-founded.

The same God who inspired Scripture is present to help you understand it. The same Holy Spirit who guided the biblical authors guides believers today as they study His Word. The same grace that saved you empowers you to grow in understanding and application of biblical truth.

As you close this book and continue your Bible study journey, carry with you the confidence that comes from knowing you're well-equipped for the adventure ahead. You have practical methods that work, solid principles that guide accurate interpretation, and the assurance that God delights to reveal Himself to those who seek Him through His Word.

The Bible, which once seemed overwhelming, is now your trusted companion for spiritual growth and development. The confusion you once felt has been replaced by competence. The intimidation you experienced has given way to anticipation for what God will teach you next.

The Ethiopian went on his way rejoicing because he finally understood God's Word. You can go on your way rejoicing too, knowing that God's Word is a lamp unto your feet and a light unto your path—not just for others, but for you.

You can do this. And with God's help and the tools you've acquired, you will.

"The entrance of thy words giveth light; it giveth understanding unto the simple" (Psalm 119:130).

Welcome to a lifetime of walking in His light.

* * *

Reviews Help Others Discover God's Word!
Did this book help you grow in confidence with Bible study?

If "Making The Bible Clear" helped you move from confusion to understanding, or gave you practical tools for studying Scripture, I'd be deeply grateful if you'd leave a brief review wherever you purchased this book.

Whether you bought it on Amazon, Barnes & Noble, Books-A-Million, your local bookstore, or any other retailer, your honest feedback helps other believers who are struggling with Bible study discover this resource.

Just a few sentences about how the LIGHT method or other concepts helped you would make a real difference. Did it change your daily Bible reading? Help you understand difficult passages? Give you confidence to share Scripture with others?

"As iron sharpeneth iron; so a man sharpeneth the countenance of his

friend" (Proverbs 27:17).

Your review sharpens the spiritual growth of other believers by helping them find tools for spiritual growth—no matter where they shop for books.

Thank you for reading, and may God continue to bless your journey in His Word!

— Pastor Jay McCaig

P.S. - Want to stay connected for future Bible study resources and encouragement? Follow me on Facebook at https://www.facebook.com/jay.mccaig for updates on upcoming books, daily inspirational content, and practical Bible study tips. I'd love to continue this journey of growing in God's Word together!

Appendix A: Recommended Bible Reading Plans for Beginners

The following reading plans are designed to help new Bible students build confidence and familiarity with Scripture while avoiding the overwhelming feeling that often comes from attempting to read the entire Bible too quickly. Each plan focuses on building understanding gradually and developing sustainable reading habits.

Getting Started: 30-Day Plans for Each Section of Scripture

These shorter plans help you become familiar with different types of biblical literature without making overwhelming commitments. Complete one plan before moving to the next, or repeat particularly helpful plans.

30-Day Gospel Introduction Plan

Purpose: Learn about Jesus' life, teachings, and mission through the most accessible Gospel.

Method: Read one chapter per day, using the LIGHT method for deeper study.

1. John 1 – The Word Became Flesh
2. John 2 – First Miracle and Temple Cleansing
3. John 3 – Nicodemus and Being Born Again
4. John 4 – The Woman at the Well

5. John 5 – Healing at the Pool
6. John 6 – Feeding 5000 and Bread of Life
7. John 7 – Teaching at the Feast
8. John 8 – Light of the World
9. John 9 – Healing the Blind Man
10. John 10 – The Good Shepherd
11. John 11 – Raising Lazarus
12. John 12 – Triumphal Entry
13. John 13 – Washing the Disciples' Feet
14. John 14 – The Way, Truth, and Life
15. John 15 – The Vine and Branches
16. John 16 – Promise of the Holy Spirit
17. John 17 – Jesus' High Priestly Prayer
18. John 18 – Arrest and Trial
19. John 19 – Crucifixion
20. John 20 – Resurrection
21. John 21 – Restoration of Peter
22. Mark 1 – Jesus' Ministry Begins
23. Mark 2 – Authority to Forgive
24. Mark 4 – Parables of the Kingdom
25. Mark 5 – Healing and Deliverance
26. Mark 8 – Who Do You Say I Am?
27. Mark 10 – Greatest in the Kingdom
28. Mark 14 – The Last Supper
29. Mark 15 – The Crucifixion
30. Mark 16 – The Resurrection

30-Day Psalm and Proverbs Plan
Purpose: Experience biblical poetry and practical wisdom for daily living.
Method: Read one psalm and one section of Proverbs each day.

1. Psalm 1 & Proverbs 1:1-19
2. Psalm 8 & Proverbs 1:20-33

3. Psalm 19 & Proverbs 2:1-15
4. Psalm 23 & Proverbs 2:16-22
5. Psalm 25 & Proverbs 3:1-18
6. Psalm 27 & Proverbs 3:19-35
7. Psalm 32 & Proverbs 4:1-19
8. Psalm 34 & Proverbs 4:20-27
9. Psalm 37 & Proverbs 5:1-14
10. Psalm 40 & Proverbs 5:15-23
11. Psalm 42 & Proverbs 6:1-19
12. Psalm 46 & Proverbs 6:20-35
13. Psalm 51 & Proverbs 7:1-27
14. Psalm 63 & Proverbs 8:1-21
15. Psalm 73 & Proverbs 8:22-36
16. Psalm 84 & Proverbs 9:1-18
17. Psalm 90 & Proverbs 10:1-16
18. Psalm 91 & Proverbs 10:17-32
19. Psalm 103 & Proverbs 11:1-15
20. Psalm 107 & Proverbs 11:16-31
21. Psalm 119:1-32 & Proverbs 12:1-14
22. Psalm 119:33-64 & Proverbs 12:15-28
23. Psalm 119:65-96 & Proverbs 13:1-12
24. Psalm 119:97-128 & Proverbs 13:13-25
25. Psalm 119:129-176 & Proverbs 14:1-18
26. Psalm 121 & Proverbs 14:19-35
27. Psalm 139 & Proverbs 15:1-17
28. Psalm 143 & Proverbs 15:18-33
29. Psalm 145 & Proverbs 16:1-16
30. Psalm 150 & Proverbs 16:17-33

30-Day New Testament Letters Plan

Purpose: Learn practical Christian living from the apostles' teachings.

Method: Read complete shorter letters and selections from longer ones.

1. James 1 – Faith and Trials
2. James 2 – Faith and Works
3. James 3 – Taming the Tongue
4. James 4 – Submit to God
5. James 5 – Patience and Prayer
6. 1 Peter 1 – Living Hope
7. 1 Peter 2 – Living Stones
8. 1 Peter 3 – Wives and Husbands
9. 1 Peter 4 – Suffering for Christ
10. 1 Peter 5 – Humility and Trust
11. 1 John 1 – Fellowship with God
12. 1 John 2 – Walking in Light
13. 1 John 3 – Children of God
14. 1 John 4 – God is Love
15. 1 John 5 – Faith Overcomes
16. Philippians 1 – Joy in Suffering
17. Philippians 2 – Humility of Christ
18. Philippians 3 – Knowing Christ
19. Philippians 4 – Peace and Contentment
20. Ephesians 1 – Spiritual Blessings
21. Ephesians 2 – Saved by Grace
22. Ephesians 3 – Mystery Revealed
23. Ephesians 4 – Unity in the Body
24. Ephesians 5 – Walking in Love
25. Ephesians 6 – Spiritual Warfare
26. Colossians 1 – Supremacy of Christ
27. Colossians 2 – Fullness in Christ
28. Colossians 3 – New Life in Christ
29. Colossians 4 – Christian Living
30. 2 Timothy 3 – Scripture's Authority

30-Day Old Testament Stories Plan

Purpose: Learn foundational stories that illustrate God's character and ways.

Method: Read complete narratives, focusing on what each teaches about God.

1. Genesis 1–2 – Creation
2. Genesis 3 – The Fall
3. Genesis 6–9 – Noah and the Flood
4. Genesis 12 – God's Call to Abraham
5. Genesis 15 – God's Covenant with Abraham
6. Genesis 22 – Abraham's Test
7. Genesis 25, 27 – Jacob and Esau
8. Genesis 28 – Jacob's Ladder
9. Genesis 37 – Joseph's Dreams
10. Genesis 39 – Joseph's Integrity
11. Genesis 41 – Joseph Interprets Dreams
12. Genesis 45 – Joseph Reveals Himself
13. Genesis 50 – Joseph's Forgiveness
14. Exodus 3–4 – Moses' Calling
15. Exodus 12 – The Passover
16. Exodus 14 – Crossing the Red Sea
17. Exodus 20 – The Ten Commandments
18. Numbers 13–14 – The Spies' Report
19. Joshua 1 – Joshua's Commission
20. Joshua 6 – The Battle of Jericho
21. Judges 6–7 – Gideon's Victory
22. Ruth 1 – Ruth's Loyalty
23. Ruth 4 – Ruth's Redemption
24. 1 Samuel 3 – Samuel's Calling
25. 1 Samuel 16 – David's Anointing
26. 1 Samuel 17 – David and Goliath
27. 2 Samuel 7 – God's Covenant with David
28. 1 Kings 18 – Elijah on Mount Carmel
29. 2 Kings 5 – Naaman's Healing

30. Daniel 3 - The Fiery Furnace

Topical Reading Plans

These plans help you understand what the Bible teaches about important life topics. Use your concordance to find additional verses on each topic.

30-Day Prayer and Faith Plan
Week 1: Learning to Pray

- Day 1: Matthew 6:5-15 (The Lord's Prayer)
- Day 2: Luke 11:1-13 (Ask, Seek, Knock)
- Day 3: Luke 18:1-8 (Persistent Prayer)
- Day 4: John 14:12-14 (Praying in Jesus' Name)
- Day 5: Ephesians 6:18 (Praying Always)
- Day 6: 1 Thessalonians 5:17 (Pray Without Ceasing)
- Day 7: James 5:13-18 (Prayer of Faith)

Week 2: Examples of Faith

- Day 8: Hebrews 11:1-6 (Definition of Faith)
- Day 9: Hebrews 11:7-12 (Noah and Abraham's Faith)
- Day 10: Hebrews 11:17-22 (Abraham and Isaac's Faith)
- Day 11: Hebrews 11:23-29 (Moses' Faith)
- Day 12: Hebrews 11:30-40 (Heroes of Faith)
- Day 13: Matthew 8:5-13 (Centurion's Faith)
- Day 14: Matthew 15:21-28 (Canaanite Woman's Faith)

Week 3: Trusting God's Provision

- Day 15: Matthew 6:25-34 (Don't Worry)
- Day 16: Philippians 4:6-7 (Peace Through Prayer)
- Day 17: Philippians 4:19 (God Will Supply)
- Day 18: Psalm 23 (The Lord is My Shepherd)

- Day 19: Psalm 37:25 (Never Seen the Righteous Forsaken)
- Day 20: 2 Corinthians 9:8 (God's Abundant Grace)
- Day 21: 1 Peter 5:7 (Cast Your Cares on Him)

Week 4: Growing in Faith

- Day 22: Romans 10:17 (Faith Comes by Hearing)
- Day 23: Romans 1:17 (The Just Shall Live by Faith)
- Day 24: 2 Corinthians 5:7 (Walk by Faith)
- Day 25: Galatians 2:20 (Live by Faith)
- Day 26: Ephesians 2:8-9 (Saved by Faith)
- Day 27: 1 John 5:4 (Faith Overcomes the World)
- Day 28: James 1:3 (Testing Produces Patience)
- Day 29: James 2:17 (Faith Without Works is Dead)
- Day 30: Jude 20 (Building Up Your Faith)

30-Day Love and Relationships Plan
Week 1: God's Love for Us

- Day 1: John 3:16 (God So Loved the World)
- Day 2: Romans 5:8 (God Demonstrates His Love)
- Day 3: 1 John 4:9-10 (God's Love Revealed)
- Day 4: 1 John 4:16 (God is Love)
- Day 5: Jeremiah 31:3 (Everlasting Love)
- Day 6: Ephesians 3:17-19 (Know Christ's Love)
- Day 7: Romans 8:35-39 (Nothing Separates Us)

Week 2: Loving God

- Day 8: Matthew 22:37-38 (Greatest Commandment)
- Day 9: John 14:15 (If You Love Me, Keep My Commandments)
- Day 10: John 14:21 (He Who Loves Me)
- Day 11: 1 John 5:3 (This is Love)

- Day 12: Deuteronomy 6:5 (Love with All Your Heart)
- Day 13: 1 Corinthians 8:3 (If Anyone Loves God)
- Day 14: James 1:12 (Crown of Life for Those Who Love)

Week 3: Loving Others

- Day 15: Matthew 22:39 (Love Your Neighbor)
- Day 16: John 13:34-35 (New Commandment)
- Day 17: 1 Corinthians 13:1-8 (Love is Patient and Kind)
- Day 18: 1 Corinthians 13:9-13 (Love Never Fails)
- Day 19: 1 John 4:7-8 (Let Us Love One Another)
- Day 20: 1 John 4:20-21 (Love God and Brother)
- Day 21: Romans 12:10 (Love One Another with Brotherly Affection)

Week 4: Practical Love in Relationships

- Day 22: Ephesians 5:22-33 (Husbands and Wives)
- Day 23: Ephesians 6:1-4 (Children and Parents)
- Day 24: 1 Peter 3:1-7 (Husbands and Wives)
- Day 25: Matthew 5:44 (Love Your Enemies)
- Day 26: Luke 6:27-36 (Do Good to Those Who Hate You)
- Day 27: Romans 12:14-21 (Overcome Evil with Good)
- Day 28: Galatians 6:2 (Bear One Another's Burdens)
- Day 29: Hebrews 13:1 (Let Brotherly Love Continue)
- Day 30: 1 Peter 4:8 (Love Covers Sins)

Chronological Reading Plans

These plans help you understand the timeline of biblical events and see how God's plan unfolds throughout history.

90-Day Old Testament Overview

Read major passages in the order of events that occurred in history.

Creation to Abraham (Days 1-15)

- Days 1-3: Genesis 1-11 (Creation, Fall, Flood, Babel)
- Days 4-9: Job 1-42 (possibly contemporary with patriarchs)
- Days 10-15: Genesis 12-25 (Abraham and Isaac)

Patriarchs to Egypt (Days 16-30)

- Days 16-21: Genesis 25-36 (Jacob and Esau)
- Days 22-30: Genesis 37-50 (Joseph in Egypt)

Exodus to Conquest (Days 31-45)

- Days 31-36: Exodus 1-20 (Moses and the Law)
- Days 37-39: Leviticus 16, 23, 26 (Key ceremonial laws)
- Days 40-42: Numbers 13-14, 20-25 (Wilderness wanderings)
- Days 43-45: Deuteronomy 1-8, 28-30 (Moses' final words)

Conquest to Kingdom (Days 46-60)

- Days 46-48: Joshua 1-6, 23-24 (Conquering the land)
- Days 49-51: Judges 2-3, 6-7, 13-16 (Period of judges)
- Days 52-54: Ruth 1-4 (Hope during dark times)
- Days 55-57: 1 Samuel 1-3, 8-10, 16-17 (Samuel and Saul)
- Days 58-60: 2 Samuel 5-7, 11-12 (David's reign)

Kingdom to Exile (Days 61-75)

- Days 61-63: 1 Kings 3, 8, 11-12 (Solomon and division)
- Days 64-66: 1 Kings 17-19, 2 Kings 2, 4-5 (Elijah and Elisha)
- Days 67-69: 2 Kings 17, 22-25 (Fall of kingdoms)
- Days 70-72: Daniel 1-3, 6 (Exile in Babylon)
- Days 73-75: Ezra 1-3, Nehemiah 1-2, 8 (Return from exile)

Wisdom and Prophecy (Days 76-90)

- Days 76-78: Selected Psalms (1, 19, 23, 51, 90, 103, 119:1-48)
- Days 79-81: Proverbs 1-3, 10-11, 31 (Practical wisdom)
- Days 82-84: Isaiah 6, 9, 40, 53, 55 (Major prophetic themes)
- Days 85-87: Jeremiah 1, 18, 31 (Judgment and hope)
- Days 88-90: Ezekiel 36-37, Malachi 3-4 (Future restoration)

60-Day New Testament Chronological Plan
Life of Christ (Days 1-30)

- Days 1-2: Luke 1-2 (Birth narratives)
- Days 3-7: Matthew 3-7 (Early ministry and Sermon on the Mount)
- Days 8-12: Luke 9-10, Matthew 13 (Ministry and parables)
- Days 13-17: John 6, 8, 10, 11 (Signs and teachings)
- Days 18-22: Matthew 16-20 (Journey to Jerusalem)
- Days 23-25: John 13-17 (Upper room discourse)
- Days 26-28: Matthew 26-27, Luke 23 (Crucifixion)
- Days 29-30: Luke 24, John 20-21 (Resurrection)

Early Church (Days 31-60)

- Days 31-35: Acts 1-5 (Church begins)
- Days 36-40: Acts 6-12 (Persecution and growth)
- Days 41-45: Acts 13-16 (Paul's first missionary journeys)
- Days 46-50: Galatians, 1-2 Thessalonians (Early letters)
- Days 51-55: 1-2 Corinthians, Romans (Major theology)
- Days 56-60: Ephesians, Philippians, Colossians, Philemon (Prison letters)

Reading Plan Guidelines

How to Use These Plans Successfully:

1. **Start Small**: Choose one 30-day plan rather than attempting a longer commitment initially.
2. **Be Consistent**: Read every day, even if you have to shorten the passage. Consistency matters more than perfection.
3. **Use the LIGHT Method**: Apply Learn, Interpret, Grow, Hear, Trust to at least one passage each week for deeper study.
4. **Keep a Journal**: Write down one thing you learned or one way you want to apply what you read.
5. **Don't Rush**: If a plan becomes overwhelming, slow down or repeat sections rather than quitting.
6. **Seek Help**: When you encounter difficult passages, use your study resources or ask for help from mature believers.
7. **Be Flexible**: Adjust plans as needed to accommodate your schedule and spiritual needs.
8. **Celebrate Progress**: Acknowledge when you complete a plan and reflect on what you've learned.

Remember: The goal isn't to finish a plan but to know God better through His Word. Let these plans serve your relationship with God, not become burdens that discourage you from Bible reading.

Appendix B: Quick Reference Guide

This appendix provides essential information for quick reference during your Bible study. Keep this section handy as you develop your study skills and biblical knowledge.

Books of the Bible in Order

Old Testament (39 Books)

The Law (5 Books)

1. **Genesis** – Creation, fall, patriarchs, and Joseph in Egypt
2. **Exodus** – Israel's deliverance from Egypt and receiving the Law
3. **Leviticus** – Laws for worship, sacrifice, and holy living
4. **Numbers** – Wilderness wanderings and preparation for the Promised Land
5. **Deuteronomy** – Moses' final speeches and review of the Law

Historical Books (12 Books)

6. **Joshua** – Conquest and division of the Promised Land
7. **Judges** – The period of judges before Israel had kings
8. **Ruth** – Story of loyalty and redemption during the judges period
9. **1 Samuel** – Samuel's ministry, Saul's reign, David's anointing
10. **2 Samuel** – David's reign as king over Israel
11. **1 Kings** – Solomon's reign and kingdom's division
12. **2 Kings** – Divided kingdom through exile
13. **1 Chronicles** – David's reign from a priestly perspective

14. **2 Chronicles** – Solomon through the exile, focusing on Judah
15. **Ezra** – Return from exile and rebuilding the temple
16. **Nehemiah** – Rebuilding Jerusalem's walls and spiritual renewal
17. **Esther** – God's providence in preserving His people in exile

Poetry and Wisdom (5 Books)

18. **Job** – Suffering, sovereignty, and faith in difficult times
19. **Psalms** – Songs and prayers expressing worship and emotion
20. **Proverbs** – Practical wisdom for daily living
21. **Ecclesiastes** – The meaning of life and the vanity of worldly pursuits
22. **Song of Solomon** – Love poetry celebrating marriage

Major Prophets (5 Books)

23. **Isaiah** – Judgment and salvation; many Messianic prophecies
24. **Jeremiah** – Warnings before exile and promises of restoration
25. **Lamentations** – Mourning over Jerusalem's destruction
26. **Ezekiel** – Visions of judgment and future restoration
27. **Daniel** – Faithfulness in exile and prophetic visions

Minor Prophets (12 Books)

28. **Hosea** – God's faithful love despite Israel's unfaithfulness
29. **Joel** – Locust plague and the Day of the Lord
30. **Amos** – Social justice and coming judgment
31. **Obadiah** – Judgment on Edom for pride and violence
32. **Jonah** – God's mercy extends to all nations
33. **Micah** – Judgment and hope; the coming Messiah
34. **Nahum** – God's judgment on Nineveh
35. **Habakkuk** – Wrestling with questions about God's justice
36. **Zephaniah** – The Day of the Lord and restoration
37. **Haggai** – Rebuilding the temple after exile
38. **Zechariah** – Encouragement for rebuilding and Messianic hope
39. **Malachi** – Call to repentance and promise of Messiah's coming

New Testament (27 Books)

Gospels (4 Books)

1. **Matthew** - Jesus as King and Messiah, written for a Jewish audience
2. **Mark** - Jesus as Servant, emphasizing His actions and power
3. **Luke** - Jesus as perfect Man, emphasizing His compassion
4. **John** - Jesus as Son of God, emphasizing His deity

History (1 Book)

5. **Acts** - The early church and spread of the gospel

Paul's Letters (13 Books)

6. **Romans** - Comprehensive explanation of the gospel and Christian living
7. **1 Corinthians** - Correcting problems in the Corinthian church
8. **2 Corinthians** - Paul's defense of his ministry and reconciliation
9. **Galatians** - Salvation by grace through faith, not works
10. **Ephesians** - The church as the body of Christ
11. **Philippians** - Joy and contentment in Christ
12. **Colossians** - The supremacy and sufficiency of Christ
13. **1 Thessalonians** - Christian living and Christ's return
14. **2 Thessalonians** - Correction about Christ's second coming
15. **1 Timothy** - Instructions for church leadership and ministry
16. **2 Timothy** - Paul's final letter, emphasizing faithfulness
17. **Titus** - Qualifications for church leaders and godly living
18. **Philemon** - Forgiveness and restoration (slavery context)

General Letters (8 Books)

19. **Hebrews** - Christ's superiority to the Old Testament system
20. **James** - Practical Christian living and faith with works
21. **1 Peter** - Hope and perseverance through suffering
22. **2 Peter** - Warning against false teachers
23. **1 John** - Assurance of salvation and walking in love
24. **2 John** - Warning against false teachers (to a lady)
25. **3 John** - Encouragement in hospitality (to Gaius)

26. **Jude** - Contending for the faith against false teachers

Prophecy (1 Book)

27. **Revelation** - Christ's victory and the end times

Key Bible Study Questions

Use these questions with any passage to guide your observation and interpretation:

LIGHT Method Questions

Learn: What does the passage say?

- What are the keywords and phrases?
- What is the main topic or theme?
- What stands out as important or unusual?
- What is repeated or emphasized?

Interpret: What does the passage mean?

- Who wrote this and to whom?
- What was the historical and cultural context?
- What type of literature is this?
- How does this fit with the surrounding context?
- What was the author's intended meaning?

Grow: How should this change my life?

- What does this teach me about God?
- What does this reveal about human nature?
- Is there a sin to confess or avoid?
- Is there a promise to claim?
- Is there a command to obey?

- Is there an example to follow or avoid?

Hear: What is the Spirit saying to me?

- How is God speaking to my heart through this passage?
- What spiritual truth is being revealed?
- How does this connect to my current circumstances?
- What is God calling me to understand or do?

Trust: How will I respond in faith and obedience?

- What specific action will I take?
- How will I apply this truth this week?
- What changes need to happen in my thinking or behavior?
- How can I trust God more fully based on this passage?

Additional Study Questions
Observation Questions

- What do I see? (people, places, events, ideas)
- What words or phrases are repeated?
- What contrasts or comparisons appear?
- What causes and effects are mentioned?
- What questions does this passage raise?

Interpretation Questions

- What did this mean to the original readers?
- How does this relate to other Scripture?
- What is the author's main point?
- How does this fit into the book's overall message?
- What cultural background helps explain this passage?

Application Questions

- How does this apply to my relationship with God?
- How does this affect my relationships with others?
- What attitudes need to change?
- What actions should I take?
- How can I share this truth with others?

Common Abbreviations and Terms

Biblical Books (Standard Abbreviations)

Old Testament: Gen., Ex., Lev., Num., Deut., Josh., Judg., Ruth, 1 Sam., 2 Sam., 1 Kings, 2 Kings, 1 Chron., 2 Chron., Ezra, Neh., Esth., Job, Ps., Prov., Eccl., Song, Isa., Jer., Lam., Ezek., Dan., Hos., Joel, Amos, Obad., Jonah, Mic., Nah., Hab., Zeph., Hag., Zech., Mal.

New Testament: Matt., Mark, Luke, John, Acts, Rom., 1 Cor., 2 Cor., Gal., Eph., Phil., Col., 1 Thess., 2 Thess., 1 Tim., 2 Tim., Titus, Philem., Heb., James, 1 Pet., 2 Pet., 1 John, 2 John, 3 John, Jude, Rev.

Study Terms

Canon - The collection of books accepted as genuine Scripture

Concordance - Alphabetical index of Bible words showing every occurrence

Cross-reference - Other Bible verses that relate to the passage being studied

Exegesis - Drawing meaning out of the text (proper interpretation)

Eisegesis - Reading meaning into the text (improper interpretation)

Genre - Type of literature (narrative, poetry, prophecy, etc.)

Hermeneutics - The science and art of biblical interpretation

Manuscript - Hand-written copies of biblical texts

Parallel passage - Different accounts of the same event or teaching

Textual criticism - Study of ancient manuscripts to determine original text

Theological Terms

Atonement - Christ's sacrificial death paying for sin

Covenant - Formal agreement or relationship between God and people

Dispensation - Period of time in God's dealings with humanity

Eschatology - Study of last things (end times)

Grace - God's unmerited favor toward sinners

Justification - God declaring sinners righteous through faith in Christ

Propitiation - Christ's death satisfying God's wrath against sin

Redemption - Being purchased or bought back from sin's bondage

Regeneration - Spiritual rebirth; being born again

Sanctification - Process of being made holy; spiritual growth

Soteriology - Study of salvation

Theology - Study of God and divine things

Timeline of Bible Events

Old Testament Timeline (Approximate Dates)

Creation to Flood (Dates uncertain)

- Creation: Genesis 1-2
- Fall: Genesis 3
- Flood: Genesis 6-9

Patriarchal Period (2000-1500 BC)

- 2000 BC: Abraham called (Genesis 12)
- 1900 BC: Isaac born (Genesis 21)
- 1800 BC: Jacob and Joseph (Genesis 25-50)
- 1700 BC: Israel enters Egypt (Genesis 46)

Exodus and Wilderness (1500-1400 BC)

- 1450 BC: Exodus from Egypt (Exodus 1-15)
- 1450 BC: Law given at Sinai (Exodus 19-24)
- 1410 BC: Wilderness wandering ends (Numbers-Deuteronomy)

Conquest and Judges (1400-1000 BC)

- 1400 BC: Conquest begins (Joshua)
- 1350-1050 BC: Period of Judges (Judges, Ruth)

United Kingdom (1050-930 BC)

- 1050 BC: Saul becomes king (1 Samuel 8-10)
- 1010 BC: David becomes king (2 Samuel)
- 970 BC: Solomon becomes king (1 Kings 1-11)
- 930 BC: Kingdom divides (1 Kings 12)

Divided Kingdom (930-586 BC)

- 930-722 BC: Israel and Judah exist separately
- 722 BC: Assyria conquers Israel (2 Kings 17)
- 605-586 BC: Babylon conquers Judah (2 Kings 24-25)

Exile and Return (586-400 BC)

- 586-538 BC: Babylonian exile (Daniel)
- 538 BC: First return under Zerubbabel (Ezra 1-6)
- 458 BC: Second return under Ezra (Ezra 7-10)
- 445 BC: Third return under Nehemiah (Nehemiah)

Inter-testamental Period (400-4 BC)

- Persian, Greek, and Roman rule
- No biblical revelation during this period

- Development of synagogues and scribal traditions

New Testament Timeline
  Life of Christ (4 BC - 30 AD)

- 4 BC: Jesus born (Matthew 1-2, Luke 1-2)
- 30 AD: Jesus' ministry begins (Matthew 3, Mark 1, Luke 3, John 1)
- 30-33 AD: Public ministry (Gospels)
- 33 AD: Crucifixion and resurrection (Matthew 26-28, etc.)

Early Church (30-100 AD)

- 33 AD: Church empowered by the Holy Spirit on Pentecost (Acts 2)
- 35 AD: Paul's conversion (Acts 9)
- 47-57 AD: Paul's missionary journeys (Acts 13-21)
- 64 AD: Nero's persecution begins
- 70 AD: Jerusalem destroyed by Romans
- 95 AD: Revelation written

Key Verses for Essential Doctrines

Salvation

- "For all have sinned, and come short of the glory of God" (Romans 3:23)
- "For the wages of sin is death; but the gift of God is eternal life through Jesus Christ our Lord" (Romans 6:23)
- "But God commendeth his love toward us, in that, while we were yet sinners, Christ died for us" (Romans 5:8)
- "For by grace are ye saved through faith; and that not of yourselves: it is the gift of God: Not of works, lest any man should boast" (Ephesians 2:8-9)

Scripture

- "All scripture is given by inspiration of God, and is profitable for doctrine, for reproof, for correction, for instruction in righteousness" (2 Timothy 3:16)
- "For the prophecy came not in old time by the will of man: but holy men of God spake as they were moved by the Holy Ghost" (2 Peter 1:21)
- "Thy word is a lamp unto my feet, and a light unto my path" (Psalm 119:105)

God's Character

- "God is a Spirit: and they that worship him must worship him in spirit and in truth" (John 4:24)
- "He that loveth not knoweth not God; for God is love" (1 John 4:8)
- "Holy, holy, holy, is the Lord of hosts: the whole earth is full of his glory" (Isaiah 6:3)
- "The Lord is not slack concerning his promise, as some men count slackness; but is longsuffering to us-ward, not willing that any should perish, but that all should come to repentance" (2 Peter 3:9)

Christian Living

- "Trust in the Lord with all thine heart; and lean not unto thine own understanding. In all thy ways acknowledge him, and he shall direct thy paths" (Proverbs 3:5-6)
- "Be ye therefore perfect, even as your Father which is in heaven is perfect" (Matthew 5:48)
- "I can do all things through Christ which strengtheneth me" (Philippians 4:13)
- "But seek ye first the kingdom of God, and his righteousness; and all these things shall be added unto you" (Matthew 6:33)

Bible Study Helps Quick Reference

When You Need Encouragement

- Psalm 23, 27, 46, 103, 139
- Isaiah 40:28-31, 41:10
- Romans 8:28-39
- 2 Corinthians 4:16-18
- Philippians 4:4-8

When You're Struggling with Sin

- Psalm 32, 51
- Romans 6:1-14, 8:1-4
- 1 Corinthians 10:13
- 1 John 1:9, 2:1-2

When You Need Wisdom

- Proverbs 1:7, 3:5-6, 9:10
- James 1:5-8
- 1 Corinthians 1:18-31

When You're Worried

- Matthew 6:25-34
- Philippians 4:6-7
- 1 Peter 5:7

When You Need to Understand God's Will

- Romans 12:1-2
- Ephesians 5:15-17

- Colossians 3:15-17

When You're Facing Trials

- Romans 5:3-5
- James 1:2-4
- 1 Peter 1:6-7, 4:12-16

Study Tools Priority List

1. **King James Bible** (primary study Bible with cross-references)
2. **Strong's Concordance** (word studies and original language helps)
3. **Bible Dictionary** (historical and cultural background)
4. **Reliable Commentary** (Matthew Henry, H.L. Willmington, or Warren Wiersbe)
5. **Bible Atlas** (geographical context)

Quick Interpretation Checklist

- [ ] Read the passage multiple times
- [ ] Identify the type of literature (genre)
- [ ] Consider the immediate context (surrounding verses)
- [ ] Research the historical/cultural background
- [ ] Look for cross-references and parallel passages
- [ ] Determine the author's intended meaning
- [ ] Apply universal principles to modern life
- [ ] Check interpretation against clear biblical teaching

Remember: "Study to shew thyself approved unto God, a workman that needeth not to be ashamed, rightly dividing the word of truth" (2 Timothy 2:15).

Appendix C: Troubleshooting Common Problems

Every Bible student encounters obstacles that can derail their study habits or discourage their spiritual growth. This appendix provides practical solutions to the most common problems beginners face, helping you overcome challenges and maintain momentum in your Bible study journey.

"I Don't Have Time"

This is the most common excuse for inconsistent Bible study, and it's often a genuine concern in our busy world. Here are practical solutions:

Realistic Time Assessment

Challenge: Feeling like you need large blocks of time to study effectively.

Solution: Start with what you actually have, not what you think you need.

- **5 minutes**: Read one psalm or a few verses using the LIGHT method
- **10 minutes**: Complete LIGHT study of one short passage
- **15 minutes**: Read a chapter and make basic observations
- **20+ minutes**: In-depth study with cross-references and applications

Remember: "For precept must be upon precept, precept upon precept; line upon line, line upon line; here a little, and there a little" (Isaiah 28:10). God builds our understanding gradually.

Finding Hidden Time

Challenge: Feeling like your schedule has no available slots.

Solutions: Look for existing time you could use more productively:

- **Morning routine**: Read while drinking coffee or eating breakfast
- **Commute time**: Listen to Bible audio or study at red lights
- **Lunch breaks**: Use 10-15 minutes for Bible reading
- **Waiting periods**: Doctor's offices, children's activities, early arrivals
- **Evening wind-down**: Replace 15 minutes of TV or social media
- **Weekend mornings**: Before family activities begin

Time Management Strategies

Replace, don't add: Instead of trying to add Bible study to an already packed schedule, replace less valuable activities.

Audit your time: Track how you spend time for one week. You'll likely find 15-30 minutes daily that could be redirected to Bible study.

Use transition times: Brief moments between activities can accumulate into meaningful study time.

Link to existing habits: Attach Bible reading to something you already do consistently (coffee, commute, bedtime routine).

Mobile and Audio Solutions

Digital Bibles: Keep a Bible app on your phone for unexpected free moments.

Audio Bibles: Listen while exercising, doing chores, or during commutes.

Voice notes: Record brief thoughts about passages to review later.

Study apps: Utilize apps that work offline for studying during travel or your commute.

"It's Too Hard"

Feeling overwhelmed by Scripture's complexity can discourage even sincere believers. Here's how to overcome this challenge:

Start Where You Are

Challenge: Thinking that you need to understand everything before you can benefit from anything.

Solution: Accept that Bible study is a lifelong learning process.

- Begin with clearer books like John, Philippians, or Psalms
- Use the easier-to-understand passages to build confidence
- Remember that even mature Christians continue learning
- Focus on what you do understand rather than what you don't

Biblical encouragement: "The law of the Lord is perfect, converting the soul: the testimony of the Lord is sure, making wise the simple" (Psalm 19:7).

Progressive Learning Strategy

Week 1-2: Read familiar stories (Psalm 23, John 3:16, Christmas/Easter narratives) **Week 3-4**: Try one chapter of John or Philippians using the LIGHT method **Month 2**: Complete study of a short book like James or 1 John **Month 3+**: Tackle slightly more challenging material

Use Study Helps Wisely

Challenge: Feeling lost without understanding historical or cultural background.

Solutions:

- Start with a study Bible that has helpful notes
- Use a Bible dictionary for unfamiliar terms or places
- Don't let lack of background knowledge stop you from reading
- Focus on the main message even when details are unclear

Simplify Your Approach

Challenge: Trying to do too much analysis at once.

Solutions:

- Use only one or two study methods initially
- Focus on observation before moving to interpretation
- Ask simple questions: What do I notice? What is the main point?
- Don't consult every available resource for every passage

Build on Success

Challenge: Getting discouraged by difficult passages.

Solutions:

- Keep a list of passages that have been meaningful to you
- Return to encouraging passages when study feels difficult
- Celebrate insights and growth, even small ones
- Remember that confusion often precedes understanding

"I Keep Forgetting What I Read"

Many Bible students struggle with retention, feeling like they're not gaining much from their reading.

Active Reading Strategies

Challenge: Passive reading that doesn't engage the mind.

Solutions:

- **Write as you read**: Take notes, underline, or highlight
- **Ask questions**: Who, what, when, where, why, how
- **Summarize**: Write one-sentence summaries of passages
- **Discuss**: Share insights with family or friends

The LIGHT Method for Retention

Learn: Writing down what you observe helps memory **Interpret**: Thinking through meaning engages your mind actively **Grow**: Personal application creates emotional connection **Hear**: Listening for God's voice makes reading spiritual, not just intellectual **Trust**: Committing to obedience reinforces what you've learned

Memory Aids

Challenge: Information goes in one ear and out the other.

Solutions:

- **Keep a study journal**: Write down insights and applications

- **Use index cards**: Record key verses or principles
- **Create connections**: Link new insights to things you already know
- **Review regularly**: Spend a few minutes weekly reviewing previous insights
- **Teach others**: Explaining what you've learned reinforces your own memory

Focus on Application
Challenge: Treating Bible study like an academic exercise.
Solution: Look for immediate ways to apply what you read.

- Ask: "How can I use this truth today?"
- Make specific commitments about attitude or behavior changes
- Pray about what you've learned
- Share applications with others for accountability

Biblical truth: "But be ye doers of the word, and not hearers only, deceiving your own selves" (James 1:22).

Cumulative Learning
Challenge: Expecting to remember everything from every study session.
Solutions:

- Understand that biblical knowledge builds gradually over time
- Focus on one main insight per study session
- Don't worry about "losing" insights—faithful study creates cumulative growth
- Trust that the Holy Spirit brings things to remembrance when needed (John 14:26)

"I'm Not Getting Anything Out of It"

Sometimes, Bible study feels dry, routine, or unrewarding despite sincere effort.

Check Your Expectations

Challenge: Expecting every study session to produce profound insights.

Reality check: Even mature Christians have ordinary study times mixed with extraordinary ones.

- Some days you're planting seeds; other days you're harvesting
- Faithful reading during dry periods often prepares your heart for future insights
- Consistency matters more than constant emotional highs
- God works through ordinary means over time

Vary Your Approach

Challenge: Bible study becoming mechanical or routine.

Solutions:

- **Change your method**: Try character studies, topical studies, or different books
- **Change your translation**: Read familiar passages in a different version
- **Change your location**: Study in a different place occasionally
- **Change your time**: If mornings aren't working, try evenings
- **Study with others**: Join a Bible study group or discuss passages with friends

Address Heart Issues

Challenge: Reading with wrong motives or attitudes.

Heart check questions:

- Am I reading to know God better or just to check off a spiritual duty?
- Am I genuinely seeking to obey what I learn?

- Am I bringing unconfessed sin that hinders spiritual perception?
- Am I relying on my own understanding instead of asking for God's help?

Biblical guidance: "If any of you lack wisdom, let him ask of God, that giveth to all men liberally, and upbraideth not; and it shall be given him" (James 1:5).

Pray for Understanding

Challenge: Forgetting that Bible study is a spiritual activity requiring God's help.

Solutions:

- Begin each study session with prayer
- Ask the Holy Spirit to open your heart and mind
- Pray about specific passages or questions
- Thank God for what He reveals, even if it seems small

Promise to claim: "Open thou mine eyes, that I may behold wondrous things out of thy law" (Psalm 119:18).

Focus on Knowing God

Challenge: Seeking information instead of relationship.

Refocus strategies:

- Ask "What does this teach me about God's character?" in every passage
- Look for reasons to worship and thank God
- Consider how the passage affects your trust in God
- Apply insights to your relationship with God, not just your behavior

Additional Troubleshooting Tips

When You Miss Days

Problem: Feeling guilty and wanting to quit after missing study days.

Solution:

- Don't try to "catch up" by doing extra reading
- Simply resume your regular schedule
- Focus on consistency over perfection
- Learn from what caused you to miss and adjust accordingly

When Family Members Don't Support Your Study

Problem: Feeling like others don't understand or support your Bible study commitment.
Solutions:

- Model the benefits through your changed attitudes and actions
- Share insights naturally without being preachy
- Include family members when appropriate
- Don't let others' lack of interest derail your commitment
- Find support from other believers who understand

When You Disagree with What You Read

Problem: Encountering passages that challenge your opinions or lifestyle.
Solutions:

- Remember that God's thoughts are higher than our thoughts (Isaiah 55:8-9)
- Pray for a submissive heart that wants to obey God's Word
- Study the passage carefully to ensure you understand it correctly
- Seek counsel from mature believers about difficult applications
- Trust that God's commands are for your good, even when they're difficult

When You Feel Spiritually Dry

Problem: Bible study feels mechanical during difficult life seasons.
Solutions:

- Continue reading even when you don't "feel" anything
- Focus on God's faithfulness rather than your feelings

- Read passages that have encouraged you in the past
- Remember that spiritual growth often happens during dry periods
- Trust that God is working even when you can't sense it

When You Have Questions That No One Can Answer

Problem: Encountering passages or concepts that remain confusing despite study and consultation.

Solutions:

- Focus on what is clear rather than what is unclear
- Trust that God will provide understanding when you need it
- Continue studying—answers often come gradually
- Hold uncertain interpretations humbly
- Don't let unanswered questions undermine your confidence in Scripture's reliability

Creating Your Personal Troubleshooting Plan

Identify Your Pattern
Common obstacles for you:

- What typically derails your Bible study?
- When are you most likely to skip study time?
- What discourages you most about Bible study?
- What external factors affect your consistency?

Develop Specific Solutions
For your top 3 obstacles, create specific action plans:

- **If this happens** (specific obstacle)
- **Then I will** (specific response)
- **Instead of** (typical negative response)

Build in Accountability
Support systems:

- Who can encourage you during difficult periods?
- Who will ask about your Bible study progress?
- What group or individual can provide guidance when you're stuck?

Regular Evaluation
Monthly assessment:

- What's working well in your Bible study?
- What obstacles did you encounter this month?
- What adjustments need to be made?
- What progress can you celebrate?

Remember God's Faithfulness

When facing any of these common problems, remember that God is more committed to your spiritual growth than you are. He promises to complete the good work He has begun in you (Philippians 1:6). Your job is to remain faithful in the small things; His job is to produce spiritual growth.

"Being confident of this very thing, that he which hath begun a good work in you will perform it until the day of Jesus Christ" (Philippians 1:6).

Every mature Christian has faced the same obstacles you're encountering. The difference between those who grow and those who give up isn't the absence of problems—it's the persistence to work through them with God's help.

Don't let temporary setbacks become permanent defeats. Use these troubleshooting strategies to overcome obstacles and maintain momentum in your Bible study journey. Remember: "And let us not be weary in well doing: for in due season we shall reap, if we faint not" (Galatians 6:9).

Appendix D: Recommended Resources

This appendix provides specific recommendations for building your Bible study library with resources that support the King James Version and align with conservative evangelical doctrine. These resources have been selected for their reliability, usefulness, and commitment to biblical authority.

"Study to shew thyself approved unto God, a workman that needeth not to be ashamed, rightly dividing the word of truth" (2 Timothy 2:15).

Study Bibles for Beginners

A good study Bible provides your foundation for serious Bible study. These recommendations offer reliable notes, helpful cross-references, and sound doctrinal perspectives.

Primary Recommendations

Scofield Reference Bible (KJV)

- **Publisher**: Oxford University Press
- **Why it's excellent**: The gold standard for dispensational Bible study. It contains extensive cross-references, helpful notes, and a clear dispensational framework. The notes are conservative and support evangelical doctrinal positions on salvation by grace, eternal security, and biblical authority.
- **Best for**: Beginners who want to understand the overall structure of Scripture and God's progressive revelation.
- **Features**: Chain references, introductions to each book, chronological

charts, and helpful appendices.

- **Note**: Available in various editions from basic to deluxe leather bindings.

Thompson Chain Reference Bible (KJV)

- **Publisher**: Kirkbride Bible Company
- **Why it's excellent**: Unique chain reference system that helps you trace topics throughout Scripture. Excellent for topical studies and understanding biblical themes.
- **Best for**: Students who learn well through topical connections and want to see how Scripture interprets Scripture.
- **Features**: 100,000 cross-references organized by topic, archaeological supplements, Bible study helps.
- **Special value**: The chain reference system teaches you to let the Bible interpret itself.

Ryrie Study Bible (KJV)

- **Publisher**: Moody Publishers
- **Why it's excellent**: Clear, concise notes that explain difficult passages without overwhelming the reader. Doctrinally sound from a dispensational perspective.
- **Best for**: Students who want helpful explanations without extensive commentary.
- **Features**: Book introductions, maps, charts, and practical study helps.

Secondary Options

Pilgrim Bible (KJV)

- **Publisher**: Oxford University Press
- **Why it's helpful**: Originally designed for conservative churches, with notes that support biblical distinctives and biblical authority.

- **Features**: Historical information, doctrinal articles, and study helps specifically designed for conservative evangelical readers.

Open Bible (KJV)

- **Publisher**: Thomas Nelson
- **Why it's useful**: Comprehensive study helps, including concordance, maps, and study articles.
- **Features**: Cyclopedic index, biblical outline, and visual aids for understanding Scripture.

Essential Reference Works

These foundational reference works support your Bible study with reliable background information and word studies.

Concordances

Strong's Exhaustive Concordance of the Bible (KJV)

- **Author**: James Strong
- **Publisher**: Various (original work now public domain)
- **Why it's indispensable**: Lists every word in the KJV with its Hebrew or Greek original. Allows you to study original language meanings without knowing Hebrew or Greek.
- **How to use**: Look up any English word to find every verse where it appears, then use the numbers to study the original language words.
- **Best editions**: Look for editions that include Strong's Hebrew and Greek dictionaries.
- **Note**: This is the single most important reference work for KJV Bible study.

Cruden's Complete Concordance (KJV)

- **Author**: Alexander Cruden
- **Why it's valuable**: Classic concordance that groups related concepts together, helpful for topical studies.
- **Advantage**: Often easier to use than Strong's for basic word studies, though less comprehensive.

Bible Dictionaries

Easton's Bible Dictionary

- **Author**: Matthew George Easton
- **Why it's excellent**: Comprehensive explanations of biblical people, places, customs, and concepts from a conservative perspective.
- **Public domain**: Available free online and in many print editions.
- **Strength**: Reliable historical and cultural information that illuminates biblical passages.

Smith's Bible Dictionary

- **Author**: William Smith
- **Why it's valuable**: Classic reference work with detailed articles on biblical topics.
- **Note**: Some editions include helpful illustrations and maps.

New Bible Dictionary

- **Publisher**: InterVarsity Press
- **Why it's recommended**: Modern scholarship with conservative perspectives.
- **Caution**: Verify that you're getting an edition that maintains conservative positions on biblical authority.

Bible Handbooks

Halley's Bible Handbook

- **Author**: Henry H. Halley
- **Why it's popular**: Provides book-by-book surveys, historical background, and archaeological information in an accessible format.
- **Strength**: Helps you understand the historical flow of Scripture and the context of each book.
- **Note**: Generally conservative, though not specifically dispensational.

Unger's Bible Handbook

- **Author**: Merrill F. Unger
- **Why it's excellent**: Conservative evangelical perspective with helpful charts, maps, and archaeological information.
- **Advantage**: Written by a scholar who maintained a firm commitment to biblical inerrancy.

Commentaries

Commentaries provide verse-by-verse explanations of Scripture. Choose carefully, as commentaries reflect their authors' theological perspectives.

Classic Commentaries

Matthew Henry's Commentary on the Whole Bible

- **Author**: Matthew Henry (1662-1714)
- **Why it's beloved**: Combines careful exegesis with practical application and devotional insight. Written from a Reformed perspective that generally aligns with evangelical doctrine on salvation and biblical

authority.

- **Strength**: Excellent for understanding both the meaning and application of passages.
- **Available**: Complete set or individual volumes, also free online.
- **Note**: Language is somewhat archaic but rewards careful reading.

John Gill's Exposition of the Entire Bible

- **Author**: John Gill (1697-1771)
- **Why it's valuable**: Written by a pastor and scholar who strongly defended biblical authority and salvation by grace alone.
- **Strength**: Thorough exposition from a conservative evangelical perspective, excellent on doctrinal passages.
- **Available**: Complete set, also free online.
- **Best for**: Students who want detailed analysis from a conservative theological framework.

Jamieson, Fausset, and Brown Commentary

- **Authors**: Robert Jamieson, A.R. Fausset, David Brown
- **Why it's respected**: Combines careful scholarship with practical application from a conservative perspective.
- **Strength**: Good balance between technical analysis and practical understanding.

Contemporary Conservative Commentaries

John Phillips Exploring Commentary Series

- **Author**: John Phillips
- **Why it's excellent**: Written from a dispensational perspective with emphasis on practical application.
- **Strength**: Clear explanation of difficult passages with attention to

conservative doctrinal distinctives.

- **Available**: Individual volumes covering most books of the Bible.
- **Note**: Particularly strong on prophecy and dispensational themes.

Oliver B. Greene Commentary Series

- **Author**: Oliver B. Greene
- **Why it's valuable**: Written by an evangelist with an emphasis on soul-winning and practical Christian living.
- **Strength**: Clear, simple explanations that emphasize the gospel and Christian growth.
- **Perspective**: Strong on salvation by grace, eternal security, and practical holiness.

Bible Knowledge Commentary

- **Editors**: John F. Walvoord and Roy B. Zuck
- **Publisher**: Victor Books
- **Why it's recommended**: Scholarly analysis from a dispensational, premillennial perspective that aligns with conservative evangelical theology.
- **Strength**: Written by Dallas Theological Seminary faculty, combining academic rigor with practical insight.
- **Available**: Old Testament and New Testament volumes.

Single-Volume Commentaries

Wycliffe Bible Commentary

- **Publisher**: Moody Press
- **Why it's useful**: Conservative evangelical perspective in a manageable single volume.
- **Strength**: Reliable basic explanations of most passages.

Believer's Bible Commentary

- **Author**: William MacDonald
- **Why it's recommended**: Clear, practical commentary from a conservative perspective with emphasis on Christian living.
- **Strength**: Good balance of explanation and application suitable for beginners.

Church History Resources

Understanding church history helps you see how Christians throughout the ages have understood and applied Scripture.

Conservative Church History

The Trail of Blood

- **Author**: J.M. Carroll
- **Why it's significant**: Presents a conservative perspective on church history, arguing for continuous succession of New Testament churches through various groups.
- **Value**: Helps conservative readers understand their heritage and the historical struggles for biblical authority.
- **Note**: Represents one conservative view of church history; read alongside other sources for broader perspective.

A History of the Baptists

- **Author**: John T. Christian
- **Why it's comprehensive**: Thorough treatment of conservative church history from an evangelical perspective.
- **Strength**: Shows how biblical churches have consistently maintained biblical principles through persecution and growth.

- **Available**: Often found in reprints through conservative publishers.

Landmark Successionism: A Crucial Question in Church History

- **Author**: G.H. Orchard
- **Why it's important**: Argues for the historical continuity of biblical principles from New Testament times.
- **Perspective**: Presents the conservative evangelical view of church history.

General Church History

Church History

- **Author**: Earle E. Cairns
- **Why it's recommended**: Evangelical perspective that respects conservative contributions to Christianity.
- **Strength**: Clear chronological presentation with attention to doctrinal developments.
- **Value**: Helps you understand how biblical interpretation has developed through church history.

Foxe's Book of Martyrs

- **Author**: John Foxe
- **Why it's classic**: Documents the persecution of Christians who maintained biblical authority against religious and political oppression.
- **Value**: Inspires faithfulness and shows the cost many paid to preserve and study Scripture.
- **Available**: Various editions, some modernized for contemporary readers.

Helpful Websites and Apps

Digital resources provide convenient access to study tools and biblical content.

Free Online Resources

Blue Letter Bible (blueletterbible.org)

- **Why it's excellent**: Comprehensive Bible study tools including multiple translations, Strong's numbers, commentaries, and original language helps.
- **KJV features**: Full KJV text with Strong's numbers, cross-references, and study tools.
- **Free resources**: Access to classic commentaries, Bible dictionaries, and study helps.

Bible Gateway (biblegateway.com)

- **Why it's popular**: Easy access to multiple Bible translations with basic study tools.
- **KJV features**: Full KJV text with basic search and cross-reference functions.
- **Study helps**: Reading plans, devotionals, and topical studies.

Bible Hub (biblehub.com)

- **Why it's valuable**: Verse-by-verse comparison of translations with access to commentaries and original language tools.
- **Strength**: Easy to compare how different translations handle specific verses.

Christian Classics Ethereal Library (ccel.org)

- **Why it's treasure**: Free access to classic Christian works including commentaries, theology books, and devotional literature.
- **Value**: Many resources recommended in this appendix are available free through this site.

Bible Apps

YouVersion Bible App

- **Why it's popular**: Free access to multiple Bible translations including KJV.
- **Features**: Reading plans, note-taking, verse sharing, and offline access.
- **Caution**: Verify the doctrinal perspective of any reading plans or devotionals.

Olive Tree Bible Software

- **Why it's useful**: Professional-level Bible study tools for mobile devices.
- **KJV resources**: Multiple KJV editions with study helps and reference works.
- **Advantage**: Can purchase and download specific conservative commentaries and reference works.

PocketBible

- **Why it's recommended**: Designed specifically for serious Bible study on mobile devices.
- **Strength**: Excellent offline capabilities and note-taking features.

Quality Bible Teachers and Authors

These teachers and authors have demonstrated commitment to biblical authority and sound doctrine over time.

Contemporary Conservative Leaders

John MacArthur (1939-2025)

- **Ministry**: Grace Community Church, Master's Seminary
- **Why he's valuable**: Commitment to verse-by-verse exposition and biblical inerrancy.
- **Resources**: "Grace to You" radio ministry, extensive commentary series, study Bible.
- **Strength**: Clear explanation of difficult passages with application to Christian living.
- **Note**: Reformed theology but generally compatible with evangelical doctrine on salvation and Scripture.

Adrian Rogers (1931-2005)

- **Ministry**: Bellevue Church, "Love Worth Finding"
- **Why he's excellent**: Clear, practical preaching that emphasizes biblical authority and conservative distinctives.
- **Resources**: Sermons, books, and study materials available through Love Worth Finding ministry.
- **Strength**: Excellent at making complex theological concepts understandable.

W.A. Criswell (1909-2002)

- **Ministry**: First Baptist Church, Dallas
- **Why he's significant**: Champion of biblical inerrancy and expository

preaching.

- **Resources**: Numerous books on Bible study, theology, and Christian living.
- **Legacy**: Influenced a generation of conservative pastors and teachers.

Paul Chappell

- **Ministry**: Lancaster Baptist Church, West Coast Baptist College
- **Why he's valuable**: Strong commitment to expository preaching, biblical inerrancy, and practical Christian living from a dispensational perspective.
- **Resources**: "Sacred Motives" series, "Growing Up" series, numerous books on Christian living and church ministry, daily devotional "Daily in the Word."
- **Strength**: Excellent at making biblical principles practical for everyday life while maintaining doctrinal depth. Particularly helpful on topics of spiritual growth, family relationships, and church leadership.
- **Note**: Combines pastoral heart with scholarly approach, emphasizing both sound doctrine and passionate evangelism in his teaching and writing.

Classic Conservative Authors

Charles Haddon Spurgeon (1834-1892)

- **Why he's beloved**: "Prince of Preachers" who combined deep biblical knowledge with passionate evangelism.
- **Resources**: Thousands of sermons, "Treasury of David" (commentary on Psalms), devotional works.
- **Strength**: Excellent at finding Christ in all Scripture and applying truth to daily life.
- **Available**: Most works free online and in various print editions.

John R. Rice (1895-1980)

- **Why he's influential**: Evangelist and author who emphasized soul-winning and biblical authority.
- **Resources**: "Sword of the Lord" publications, numerous books on Christian living and Bible study.
- **Perspective**: Strong fundamentalist stance with emphasis on evangelism.

Curtis Hutson (1934-1995)

- **Why he's respected**: Editor of "Sword of the Lord," champion of biblical inerrancy and conservative distinctives.
- **Resources**: Books on salvation, Christian living, and soul-winning.
- **Strength**: Clear presentation of gospel and emphasis on practical Christian living.

Doctrinal and Theological Resources

Lewis Sperry Chafer

- **Work**: "Systematic Theology" (8 volumes)
- **Why it's important**: Comprehensive systematic theology from dispensational perspective.
- **Strength**: Thorough treatment of major doctrines with extensive biblical support.
- **Note**: Academic level but essential for serious doctrinal study.

J. Dwight Pentecost

- **Work**: "Things to Come" (prophecy), "The Words and Works of Jesus Christ"
- **Why he's valuable**: Clear explanation of biblical prophecy and Christ's

ministry from dispensational perspective.

- **Strength**: Makes complex prophetic passages understandable.

Charles C. Ryrie

- **Works**: "Basic Theology," "Dispensationalism Today," "The Holy Spirit"
- **Why he's recommended**: Clear, systematic presentation of biblical doctrine.
- **Strength**: Excellent at explaining theological concepts in accessible language.

Basic Reference Books

These foundational reference works support serious Bible study without requiring advanced theological training.

Bible Atlases

Baker Bible Atlas

- **Why it's helpful**: Clear maps showing biblical geography with explanations of how location affected events.
- **Strength**: Helps you visualize biblical narratives and understand geographical references.

Holman Bible Atlas

- **Why it's comprehensive**: Detailed maps, photographs, and geographical information for all biblical periods.
- **Value**: Excellent for understanding the historical and geographical context of Scripture.

Archaeological Resources

Halley's Bible Handbook (mentioned above)

- **Archaeological value**: Includes significant archaeological discoveries that confirm biblical accounts.
- **Strength**: Shows how archaeology supports biblical reliability.

New Bible Dictionary

- **Archaeological articles**: Contains up-to-date archaeological information that illuminates biblical passages.
- **Caution**: Verify theological perspective of any articles touching on doctrinal issues.

Study Guides and Workbooks

Exploring the Scriptures by John Phillips

- **Why it's practical**: Workbook approach to Bible study with questions and exercises.
- **Strength**: Helps you develop your own study skills rather than just reading about them.

Jensen's Survey of the Old/New Testament

- **Author**: Irving Jensen
- **Why it's valuable**: Provides overview of each book with study questions and charts.
- **Strength**: Helps you see the big picture before studying individual passages.

Building Your Library Strategically

Phase 1: Essential Foundation (First 6 months)

1. **KJV Study Bible** (Scofield or Thompson Chain Reference)
2. **Strong's Exhaustive Concordance**
3. **Bible Dictionary** (Easton's or Smith's)
4. **Basic Commentary** (Matthew Henry or Believer's Bible Commentary)

Phase 2: Expanding Understanding (Months 7-18)

1. **Bible Handbook** (Halley's or Unger's)
2. **Bible Atlas**
3. **Conservative Commentary Series** (John Phillips or Oliver Greene)
4. **Church History** (conservative perspective)

Phase 3: Deepening Study (Year 2+)

1. **Multi-volume Commentary Set**
2. **Systematic Theology** (Chafer or Ryrie)
3. **Original Language Helps** (Vine's Dictionary, Interlinear Bible)
4. **Specialized Studies** (based on your interests and calling)

Budget-Friendly Strategies

Free Resources First

- Many classic works are available free online
- Public domain books can often be downloaded at no cost
- Libraries often have good biblical resources

Used Book Sources

- Seminary bookstores often sell used textbooks
- Online marketplaces offer significant savings
- Church libraries sometimes sell older editions

Gradual Building

- Purchase one quality resource rather than several mediocre ones
- Wait for sales from Christian publishers
- Consider digital editions which are often less expensive

Share Resources

- Bible study groups can purchase expensive resources collectively
- Seminary libraries often allow community access
- Church libraries can be enhanced through member donations

Evaluating New Resources

As you encounter new books, teachers, or digital resources, evaluate them carefully:

Doctrinal Checklist

- **Biblical Authority**: Does the resource affirm that Scripture is God's inspired, inerrant Word?
- **Salvation**: Is salvation presented as by grace through faith alone, not by works?
- **Christ's Deity**: Is Jesus presented as fully God and fully man?
- **Gospel Clarity**: Is the gospel message clear and central?

Practical Evaluation

- **Clarity**: Is the material presented in understandable language?
- **Scripture-centeredness**: Does the resource point you to Scripture rather

than human wisdom?

- **Practical Value**: Will this resource actually help your Bible study?
- **Reputation**: Is the author/publisher known for biblical faithfulness?

Conservative Distinctives to Consider

- **Church autonomy**: Does the resource respect local church independence?
- **Believer's baptism**: Is baptism presented as for believers only, by immersion?
- **Congregational polity**: Are biblical principles of church governance upheld?
- **Soul liberty**: Is individual responsibility to God emphasized?

Special Considerations for Digital Resources
Advantages of Digital Tools

- **Searchability**: Find verses, topics, or concepts instantly
- **Portability**: Carry extensive libraries on mobile devices
- **Cost**: Often less expensive than print versions
- **Updates**: Software can be updated with new features and resources

Potential Disadvantages

- **Distraction**: Digital devices can interrupt study with notifications
- **Dependence**: May reduce careful reading skills
- **Eye strain**: Extended screen time can be tiring
- **Technical issues**: Software problems can interrupt study

Best Practices for Digital Study

- Turn off notifications during study time
- Use digital tools to supplement, not replace, careful reading

- Consider using print Bibles for primary reading and digital tools for reference
- Backup important notes and highlights regularly

Conclusion: Building Wisdom Through Good Resources

"A wise man will hear, and will increase learning; and a man of understanding shall attain unto wise counsels" (Proverbs 1:5).

The goal of building a study library is not to impress others with the size of your collection but to have reliable tools that help you understand and apply God's Word more effectively. Choose resources carefully, build gradually, and remember that the best library in the world is worthless without consistent use guided by the Holy Spirit.

Start with the essentials, add resources as your needs become clear, and always prioritize quality over quantity. Most importantly, let your growing library serve your growing relationship with God through His Word.

"The simple believeth every word: but the prudent man looketh well to his going" (Proverbs 14:15). Be prudent in choosing resources, but be confident that God will use good tools in the hands of sincere students to accomplish His purposes in your life.

Remember that these resources are servants, not masters. They should enhance your understanding of Scripture, not replace your own careful study. Use them wisely, and they will serve you well throughout your lifelong journey of learning and growing in God's Word.

"Buy the truth, and sell it not; also wisdom, and instruction, and understanding" (Proverbs 23:23).